OUR STORY
Coming out in the time of HIV and AIDS

Robert Hamilton

OUR STORY ©2020 by Robert Hamilton. All rights reserved. No part of this book may be used or reproduced in any manner whatsoever without written permission except in the case of brief quotations in critical articles and reviews. For more information, contact Renaissance Press. First edition.

Cover and interior design by Nathan Fréchette.
Edited by Myryam Ladouceur and Talia C. Johnson.

Legal deposit, Library and Archives Canada, October 2020.

Paperback ISBN 978-1-987963-91-5
Ebook ISBN 978-1-987963-92-2

Renaissance Press
http://pressesrenaissancepress.ca
pressesrenaissancepress@gmail.com

OUR STORY

Coming out in the time of HIV and AIDS

CONTENT WARNING

This memoir deals with illness and death, homophobia both outwards and internalized; transphobia, incarceration and the penal system.

This memoir is set in the 1970s and 1980s, and as such, employs a lot of the language that was used back then, and may not be current right now.

Joe, Ray, and Roger;
You may be gone, but you're in my art forever.

Friends and family;
It's a beautiful thing.

Drag Queens;
You are the colour in the rainbow.

Life:
You are but queer, aren't you? Thank God.

This is but one story

My story

Among the many stories

That make up OUR STORY

About a time that was

So we don't forget

So we heal.

My choices, a career as an actor or studying fine arts, were not very realistic for a kid from a small, pulp and paper mill town in northern New Brunswick. On the other hand, the two-year Correctional Worker program offered at Centennial College in Scarborough, Ontario, was much more acceptable. When I told my mother I was interested in becoming an actor, she said she'd be too embarrassed to admit that to anyone. One day, after coming out of the woods from a day of hunting with my father and uncle, my mother's brother, I mentioned my wanting to become an actor. My father said nothing. My uncle said actors had to wear makeup and I just wanted an excuse to wear makeup. If there was any suspicion in the family of me being a fruit, and there was, becoming an actor would have confirmed it. What I knew about being a fruit was derived from what I heard around me and it was definitely not what I wanted to be. Becoming a jail guard just made the most sense.

Halloween night, October 31, 1977 - Two months into my first semester and on the eve of my eighteenth birthday, I was invited to join a few classmates going into downtown Toronto to watch an annual Halloween spectacle that was apparently a must-see and guaranteed good laugh. We caught the subway in Scarborough, hopped off at Yonge and Bloor and walked down Yonge Street to where a large crowd had gathered, directly across the street from the St. Charles Tavern, a notorious gay bar. I had no idea gay bars even existed. Although "the gay" stirred within me, my knowledge of gay was zero. There was a mob atmosphere to the crowd that was fueled by hatred and bigotry and directed at the faggots and queers taking refuge inside the gay bar. As more people gathered, the uproar from the crowd increased. A guy rode his bicycle up and down the street and fixed to the back of it was a large vendor sign advertising FRUITS. Each time the guy rode past, the mob erupted into a collective roar of laughter and approval, me along with them. When a man walking on the opposite side of the street tried to duck inside the bar, a barrage of eggs, tomatoes, and whatever else was hurled his way. The crowd in unison cheered and jeered. What intrigued me was how normal the gay guy looked. I would never have guessed he was a fruit. Keeping with Halloween tradition, a procession of drag queens was supposed to leave from the St. Charles Tavern and parade up Yonge Street; an event some queens prepared for all year long. This Halloween night, the procession of queens didn't take place for fear of the mob waiting outside the tavern's front door. Eventually, the police dispersed the crowd and we moved on, taking the subway back to Scarborough.

January, 1978 - As part of my second semester curriculum, I had a four-month field placement at the Toronto East Detention Centre, otherwise known as "The East", a new maximum security jail with the capacity to hold a few hundred prisoners. It was paramilitary and staffed with many war veterans. Consequently, there were many goons on staff and it was definitely an US versus THEM mentality. If an officer showed any hint of concern for the prisoners, he or she would be labeled a "social worker". I was definitely out of my comfort zone and in a sink or swim situation. Failure wasn't an option. I was eighteen with a baby face. Without the uniform, I would have been someone's bitch in no time. Every criminal imaginable was housed there: rapists, murderers, baby killers, arsonists, hit men, and those in for petty crimes. It didn't take long to see that monsters seldom look like monsters, but more like you and me.

During one of my early days, a fellow classmate and I were taken to the segregation unit, aka "the hole", where we were instructed on how to carry out a proper skin search. The two prisoners used as our guinea pigs were in "seg" because they were on suicide watch and would not survive one minute in general population. At the time, the two were amongst the most despised men in the prison, the city, the province, and possibly the country. A few months earlier, on July 28, the two prisoners were involved in the rape, torture and murder of twelve-year-old shoeshine boy, Emanuel Jacques. The boy was raped over a twelve-hour period and then drowned in a kitchen sink. His body, wrapped in a green garbage bag, was found a few days later on the roof above a Yonge Street body rub parlour. Their crime was front-page news and captivated the city. The men were known to have frequented the St. Charles Tavern and the gay community was viewed with guilt by association. The city and its people came down hard on the gay community because of these men's heinous crimes. When the two accused child murderers were let out of their cells, I was taken aback by how normal they looked. They didn't look like the monsters I had expected to see. Being on suicide watch, they wore heavy canvas smocks called "baby dolls". The guard in charge of the unit ordered one of the prisoners to remove his baby doll and then step by step he demonstrated how to conduct a proper skin search. Never touching the prisoner, starting at the head and working down his body, ordering him to run his fingers through his hair, show behind his ears, open his mouth, lift his tongue, lift both arms to show his armpits, lift his penis, pull back foreskin if necessary, lift his ball sac, turn around and show the soles of his feet and finally, order him to bend over and spread the cheeks of his ass so it can be seen if he's trying to "suitcase" contraband. Never before had a man stood so naked before me. When walking away I'm not sure what intrigued me most, that they were murderers or homosexuals? I would learn that many gay men around this time were falsely accused of such crimes.

Early Summer, 1979 - After successfully completing the two-year Correctional Worker program, I had no job offers, was still a virgin, and still very much in the closet. I had heard about a new remand centre opening in Edmonton. Coming from the Maritimes, the world ceased to exist beyond Toronto, so I checked for Edmonton's exact location on the map and decided to fly there and check out job prospects. On arrival, I checked into the downtown YMCA. I had danced to the song by the Village People many times, but was oblivious to its gay reference, and oblivious to the "Y" being an excellent cruising spot for gay men.

While walking down Jasper Avenue, I stopped in at a hotel smoke shop to buy junk food. When checking out the magazine rack, Blue Boy - an International Magazine for Men with a half-naked man on the cover caught my eye. I instinctively knew it was a gay porn magazine. I wanted badly to look at the photos of naked men but feared getting caught so I turned away and left. Unable to stop thinking about the gay porn magazine and after wrestling with my conscience for a few hours, I walked back and stood on the sidewalk in front of the hotel with my heart racing. When I built up enough courage, I stood inside the lobby and cased out the smoke shop. When there was no one in sight I made a mad dash inside, walked directly to the magazine rack, grabbed the Blue Boy magazine and made a beeline for the clerk standing behind the counter. He couldn't put the gay porn magazine into a paper bag fast enough. I got out of there and raced back to my room at the "Y" where I got my money's worth within the first few minutes.

I checked out the Edmonton Remand Centre and it wouldn't be in operation for a few more months. The following day, I took the Greyhound bus to Calgary and checked into a cheap motel in a seedy part of the city. At a nearby corner store I purchased another gay porn magazine. This time I was more confident and less embarrassed. Again, it only took a few minutes to get my money's worth.

I checked out the Calgary Remand Centre and Spy Hill Jail but there were no immediate job openings. I decided to return home. Leaving the motel, I was stuck with the dilemma of what to do with my two gay porn magazines. Taking them with me was definitely out of the question and so was leaving them at the motel for housekeeping to find. On the bus ride to the airport I felt like I was carrying a ticking time-bomb with me. Arriving at the airport, I went directly into the men's washroom, dumped the two gay porn magazines into the garbage can and got the hell out of there. Several hours later I was back home in northern New Brunswick.

Summer, 1979 - I worked all summer in the pulp mill. When the end of summer neared, I was soon to be out of a job and without future prospects. Then fate intervened. I received a letter from the Solicitor General's office in Alberta informing me they were interviewing for correctional officer positions for the Edmonton Remand Centre, with the interviews being held in Toronto for one week. I set up an appointment for the following week, flew to Toronto and two weeks later I was offered employment.

Fall, 1979 - While on the flight from Toronto to Edmonton, I fantasized about not getting off the airplane in Edmonton. Instead, I would keep going to Australia. I envisioned myself at the other end of the world where no one knew me, where I could be myself and possibly fall in love with a man. I knew my family would never go looking for me there. I would never contact them and eventually they would give up looking for me, thinking I was dead and possibly murdered. Landing in Edmonton, I had no choice but to disembark from the plane because it was not going any farther.

I would call Edmonton home for the next two and a half years. Edmonton was not Australia and at first, I was a stranger amongst strangers. There was no need to abandon my family after all. I was far enough beyond Toronto for them to ever visit.

Early, 1980 - The remand centre was a high-tech, maximum security provincial jail with the capacity to hold three hundred and eighty-eight prisoners. Within the first few months the prisoners quickly discovered the weak spots and there were a few escapes. The media quickly labeled it the "Edmonton Sieve".

I found a shared accommodation for the first few months and then moved into my own one-bedroom apartment in the downtown core directly across from Edmonton's CN Tower, a short walk to the remand centre. The CN tower was a wall of black glass so I could not see into any of the offices and naively presumed they could not see out. After a few months of living in my new pad, the wife of one of the correctional officers I worked and hung out with approached me. She had recently begun working in the CN Tower, working part-time with varied work days and shifts. When she first started at the office all she heard about was "The Streaker". She never saw "The Streaker" because when she was working, he wasn't home. Then one day when she was at the office, he was home. She finally got to see him. I was "The Streaker" the office workers had been entertained by for the last few months – curtains wide open and me walking around naked. With my waterbed up against the bedroom window, I was mortified to think how many times they watched me choking the chicken.

Fall/Winter, 1980 - I encountered my first two transgender women when working a midnight shift. The two ladies were charged with prostitution and with no place to house them at city cells, they were dropped off at the remand centre. Being the middle of the night, the Admit/Discharge area was closed and since I was the one on shift who most often worked in that area, I was the officer chosen to book them in. I had never met or seen a transgender person before. In the male dominated justice system, they were treated with much contempt and referred to as "trannies", "its", or "he/shes". One was white and blonde, the other Native with long black hair. Both were wrapped inside their large, full-length fur coats and a cloud of perfume wafted over them. They were definitely hot looking babes. Without prejudice, most men would be happy to have them hanging off their arm. After booking the ladies in, I escorted them to the back area where they surrendered their glamorous possessions and stripped down naked. I looked at their bodies with much curiosity. Both had big, beautiful breasts, hairless bodies, and were undeniably shaped like women. For the first time, I had two naked women standing before me. I skin searched both, starting at the top and working my way down their body. The skin search was supposed to end with me asking them to bend over and spread their cheeks, but I couldn't bring myself to do so. They were well tucked. I had not seen a penis throughout the whole procedure. While handing out their prison issue, I naively asked what part of them was actually male. They sounded surprised by my ignorance and told me they still had their penises of course, thus identifying them as male. I handed them the standard male prisoner's clothes: jeans, a white t-shirt and a jean jacket, along with women's panties and bras. Instead of men's sturdy black shoes, I gave them the women's runners. They thanked me and said I was a "sweetie".

That winter, I saw an advertisement in the newspaper for acting classes at the Citadel Theatre. I enrolled. This was my opportunity to pursue my high school dream. I was not a natural talent and no knowledge that there was a craft involved.

Spring, 1981 - I enrolled in acting classes again. This time, I was inspired to write my own play, even though I knew nothing about writing a play. But I was young, cocky, and happily ignorant. I volunteered to work midnight shifts at the remand centre. Arriving on shift, the prisoners were already locked down and my job for the following eight hours would consist of sitting in my office that looked out onto the tier, and once an hour go from cell to cell shining my flashlight inside making sure all prisoners were accounted for and breathing. This took all of five minutes. Between rounds, I sat in the office and banged out my play on an electric typewriter.

When my second round of acting classes came to an end, it was decided we'd celebrate that Saturday night at a private gay dance club called Flashback. It was "the" underground dance club in the city. I had heard the straight "cool guards" at work talking about partying there. If you were straight and partied at Flashback on the weekend that meant you were "cool". Our acting teacher was a member and able to sign us all in. The club was packed with people and energy. There were drag queens, girls with girls, boys with boys, and men in leather. It was a lot for my virgin eyes to take in. A guy asked me to dance but I politely declined. Why would I? I wasn't gay. The only one I danced with that night was with Tania, one of the girls I befriended in acting class and who would remain a long-term friend. While on the dance floor I was shocked to see two male guards from the remand centre dancing together. I had no idea they were gay. They worked a different shift, so I didn't know them personally. Now knowing where Flashback was located, I returned on my own a few Saturday nights later. I first sat inside my car working up the courage to go inside. When I made my move, I made a mad dash into the club. Inside the main door was a cashier's booth where I needed to show my membership card and pay an entrance fee before being buzzed through another door and into the club. Since I was neither a member nor a familiar face, the girl sitting inside the booth denied my entrance. But I persisted and each time I showed up the girl inside the booth turned me away.

Summer, 1981 - I began working part-time as a waiter at The Old Spaghetti Factory restaurant in downtown Edmonton. A few of the waiters on staff were gay. Eventually I would come to understand being gay and a waiter was considered cliché. Everyone loved the gays at The Old Spaghetti Factory and on Friday and Saturday nights after the restaurant closed, the remaining staff would race the few blocks over to Flashback for last call. Once the staff got to know me I was invited along and soon I became a familiar face to the girl sitting inside the booth. One Saturday night in August, when I wasn't working at the jail or restaurant, I showed up at Flashback on my own and was allowed in. Both excited and nervous, I strutted into the bar. Standing just inside the door and in front of me was a "he/she", literally half man, half woman. There was no one dominant gender. A motorcycle cap rested atop his/her mound of big hair. He/she wore lipstick and makeup and at the same time he/she had a full-grown moustache. There was hair on his/her chest but no breasts. He/she wore a leather vest, a corset, and long, black leather high-heeled boots that stopped at the upper thigh. He/she had a drink in one hand and a bullwhip in the other that he/she periodically snapped. He/she was "on" and had those around him/her laughing at his/her cutting and sharp wit. He/she was loud, animated and commanded attention as he/she passed through the crowd. No doubt he/she was a WOW moment for me. I was fascinated, captivated and confused. But that didn't stop me from taking the bartender home that night. We were the same age and both from northern New Brunswick. That night, I had sex for the first time. I felt awkward, somewhat embarrassed, and conscious of the act, but it felt right. The following afternoon, the bartender took me back to Flashback to show me off to his friends.

I was fresh meat, a new face, and a curiosity. We sat at a table and were soon joined by four of the regulars. They were impressed with me being a jail guard. It meant I was "butch". I was asked what I thought of the scene so far and said I hadn't much experience, but so far so good. Then I went on to tell them about the he/she I'd seen the night before. I told them I was okay with the he/she wanting to be a girl, but found it odd he was not fully dressed as one. The guy sitting across from me said that perhaps the he/she didn't want to be a girl, and maybe what the he/she was wearing was a costume. I was sure of what I'd seen and emphatically argued that he wanted to be a girl. The guy emphatically disagreed and insisted that it was a costume. About to continue arguing my point, I had a light bulb moment. Click. The guy sitting across from me was the he/she that I was telling him about. He smiled and nodded his head confirming that he was indeed the "he/she". It was Edmonton's Gay Pride weekend and he was in costume as part of a tough drag competition, where he took first place. I congratulated him and confessed I had never heard of tough drag or Gay Pride before. His name was Joe Butler and unknown to both of us that was the beginning of what would be a long-lasting friendship. For Joe and his drag queen friends sitting at the table that afternoon, Flashback was their playground where they got to be young, gay, and creative. Through Joe, I soon learned drag wasn't a gender confusion issue, but pure theatre.

Fall/Winter, 1981 - On subsequent returns to Flashback on the weekends I would run into Joe, often in drag, and end up hanging out with him for the night, which was always a guaranteed good laugh. One of his drag characters was Miss Jodie Jean, dressed in what he called his "Myrna fish, real girl look." She was a well-groomed career woman selling real estate. She wore sensible heels, sensible business suit, a fox stole draped over her shoulders called "Freeway" (meaning road kill), and carried a briefcase. "A girl never knows when she might have to close a deal."

March, 1982 - After a few months of getting to know Joe, he invited me to join him and his roommate Sam on a fun-filled, gay weekend in Vancouver, for Vancouver's Coronation Ball. According to Joe this was a major gay event in which the reigning Emperor and Empress of Vancouver step down after their year of rule and a new Emperor and Empress, or as Joe called them, the King and Queen of the queers, are crowned. This was part of the gay court system that existed in major cities across Canada and the United States; a monarchy made up of queens, kings, princesses, princes and their entourage. The courts are registered as non-profit societies and raise money for local charities. Just before meeting Joe, he had stepped down as Emperor of Edmonton's Imperial Sovereign Court of the Wild Rose. As former king of the Edmonton queers, Joe liked to brag of being the first Emperor to ever step down in a dress. The theme for his coronation was Atlantis and as part of his costume he wore a gold lamé skirt.

On a Friday afternoon, Joe, Sam, and I flew out of Edmonton and two hours later stood at the luggage carousel at Vancouver's airport with two six-foot-tall, burly drag queens rushing towards us calling out, "Girls! Girls!" The two queens were from Calgary and looked very much like men in drag, one of them wearing fluffy bedroom slippers. The queens were there to surprise Joe and Sam and drive us into downtown Vancouver. I stood back, said nothing, but thought "fuck me" and went along with the whole absurd scene. I expected Vancouver to be cold like Edmonton, but it was a sunny day and the lawns were a healthy green. It was love at first sight, a young city with snow-capped mountains to the north and sandy beaches along the waterfront. I was sold. The Calgary girls dropped us off at the Dufferin, the host hotel. All weekend the hotel was overrun by drag queens and proud queers. It was a continual eye opener and learned that "fish" and "trick" had whole other meanings in the gay world. That Friday night we went to the Out Of Town show to watch the out of town queens perform. Joe introduced me to several of his drag friends including Miss Tuesday Night, a popular Vancouver queen. When Joe told me Tuesday wasn't black, which she appeared to be, I didn't believe him until she raised her dress sleeve and showed me her white skin. Tuesday was actually half black, with a black mother and white father, or the other way around. The following afternoon, the hotel rooms and hallways were a flurry of drag queens scampering about as they got ready for the Coronation Ball. When we arrived at the Commodore Ballroom on Granville Street crowds of onlookers lined the sidewalks out front watching the parade of drag queens arriving, some by limousine. Unlike the crowd that I had encountered on Halloween night outside the St. Charles Tavern in Toronto, this crowd was civil. Curiosity and excitement rather than hatred filled the air. Stepping inside the Commodore Ballroom was like taking a step back in time to 1920s art deco. The room was impressive and so were the few hundred gay men there to party. Everywhere I looked there was eye candy. It was definitely sensory overload. The spectacle became even more spectacular after snorting coke and whatever else in the women's washroom with Joe and his drag queen friends. The ball was exceptional. The boys, so many and so willing to show off their hot bodies were wonderful to look at, but the night and the show truly belonged to the queens. They were the belles of the ball. While swallowing the room in with my eyes I spotted a guy a few tables over staring at me. Every time I looked his way he was staring at me. Finally, I had enough and told Joe the next time I caught him staring at me, I was going to go over and ask him what his fucking problem was. Joe laughed and informed me that the guy was "cruising" me - one more word to add to my gay dictionary. Joe said the guy was staring at me because he found me attractive. Knowing that certainly put a different spin on the story. I was flattered but not interested. I was too busy watching the entertainment and partying with the queens. The reigning Vancouver Empress stepping down that night was Oliv, a tall, lean queen, well known for her eccentricity. It was expected she'd put on a good show and she didn't disappoint. The highlights of the evening were the command performances from the top queens in the room with standout performances from Dee Dee Drew and Sandy St. Peters. Each performance was an astounding display of costumes, creativity and talent. It was definitely a night of grand theatre and unknown to us at the time, what we were reveling in was the height of drag and gay culture. After the party was over, Joe, Sam and I returned to Edmonton and our routines. No sooner were we back, Joe started talking about moving to Vancouver. I was game. My two year contract with the remand centre had expired, so I had nothing holding me back.

April, 1982 – Before making our final decision to move or not, Joe and I drove to Vancouver and hung out in the city for a week. We checked back into the Dufferin Hotel, explored the city and drove around areas where we considered living. We partied in the bars and for the first time in my life, I went to a bathhouse courtesy of Joe. For a nominal fee I was handed a towel and a key to a private room for a maximum of eight hours and access to all the sex I wanted. It sounded like money well spent. As it turned out, the sex lasted no more than a few minutes. The guy came into my room, took off his towel, touched my chest, lowered my towel, stroked his dick and I blew my load in anticipation. As I learned, the bathhouse was a "your orgasm, your problem" kind of place. No one was sticking around to finish you off. By the end of the week, Joe and I were convinced Vancouver was where we needed to be. We drove back to Edmonton, quit our jobs and by the end of May we were looking at the city of Edmonton in the rear-view mirror. We were young, full of hope, confident, and ready for a whole new gay adventure.

June 1, 1982 - Joe and I moved into the lower half of a duplex in the Mount Pleasant area. Across from us was the Mount Pleasant Community Centre where I began my new addiction, working out with weights and body building. It wasn't a great gym but an improvement over my set of weights from Canadian Tire. A few months later, I joined a gay gym near the West End called The Neighbourhood Gym. In search of a correctional officer job I mailed resumes to all the correctional facilities listed in the blue pages at the back of the telephone book. Meanwhile, I worked as a waiter at The Old Spaghetti Factory in Gastown. Joe applied for drafting jobs and while waiting for that to pan out he worked full time as a bathhouse attendant at The Club Vancouver and part-time waiter. Socially, we went in opposite directions within the gay community. He embraced the drag community and I joined the gay softball league. There was no lack of gay bars to be seen in. Joe had met a guy at the Club Vancouver bathhouse when we were previously here for the week and started dating him soon after we arrived. One night in late July, at Buddy's bar in the West End, I ran into Jean Michel, a French-Canadian flight attendant I had been having sex with. He was there with his on-again, off-again boyfriend Ted and Ted's best friend Ray, all in their early thirties. Later in the evening I noticed Jean Michel, Ted, and Ray on the other side of the bar with Ray seriously cruising the hell out of me. Ray came across as self-assured, cocky and masculine. I was attracted to him but not into playing the mating game and left the bar. A few days later, while playing softball I misjudged my slide into second base, shattered my left ankle and was hospitalized for two nights. Before and after surgery I was administered morphine every four hours for the pain. It was sweet nectar. One shot and off I went into La La Land for the next four hours. It got to where I impatiently watched the clock for the fourth hour so I could get another shot. I wanted the happy happy to never end - and then it did, when the nurse handed me two Tylenol threes, as per doctor's orders. No more happy happy. My ankle suddenly became insufferable. Two days later Jean Michel showed up to give me a ride home and handed me a large bouquet of flowers. I was embarrassed. No man had ever given me flowers before. A saving grace was with me being on crutches, Jean Michel had to carry the flowers out to the car. My broken ankle ended softball for the summer and my waiter job at The Old Spaghetti Factory.

Friday, August 13, 1982 - I ran into Ray two weeks later, again at Buddy's bar, this time with me on crutches. Ray said he had seen me earlier in the week hobbling along the sidewalk and thought of offering me a ride but then remembered me walking out on him at the bar and decided to let me keep hobbling along. I went home with Ray that night and stayed for the next two and a half years. Ray was a man's man and worked as a HVAC technician (heating, ventilation, and air conditioning), servicing commercial units. He was separated with one young daughter. He said he always fucked around with guys but never thought of himself as being gay until he fell in love with another man.

Fall, 1982 - Joe's relationship with his guy lasted only a few months. He couldn't get past Joe's dresses in the closet. After Joe's "affairette", as he called it, ended, the ex-boyfriend got a taste of a woman scorned. Joe called the hydro and phone company, claimed to be the boyfriend, told them he was moving out of his apartment at month's end and needed his phone and hydro service cut off. Joe relished in the news when he heard it through the grapevine that his plan worked.

I observed when hanging out in the "butch" man on man crowd, chumming around with drag queens was a sure way to get one's "butch points" downgraded. This was evident when hanging out with Joe in drag. It surprised me to learn that after surviving the brutality of our youth, we come out in the safety of our own community and face the same prejudice. Joe loved getting into drag, always with his signature red hair, sassy mouth, fabulous gowns, and biting wit.

I received a reply from one of the correctional facilities I'd applied to. I was given an interview and soon afterwards started working as an auxiliary correctional officer at three Lower Mainland halfway houses with one being on the grounds of the infamous Okalla prison. There was a lot of downtime working in these facilitates, so reading the daily newspaper became a regular part of my routine. This is when I first became aware of the AIDS crisis, reading about a number of gay men showing up at the hospitals in major U.S. cities, suffering from pneumonia and some from a rare form of cancer called Kaposi's sarcoma. Weeks and months passed and the news of a new "gay plague" remained a constant story.

Early, 1983 - One of the first guys I was aware of who had AIDS worked out at the Neighbourhood Gym. I remember one of the gym regulars, a gay activist, going up to the man and kissing him on the lips to show our fear of AIDS was exaggerated. Over a few short years, many of the guys from the gym would succumb to HIV and AIDS.

When I first arrived in Vancouver, I saw someone from my hometown at the Castle Pub. We grew up on the same street but he was older than me and we didn't really know each other. The last time I saw him in the Castle Pub, he didn't look at all well. With a noticeable weight loss, my guess was he had "it". I would eventually learn he was an early victim to AIDS.

Spring/Summer, 1984 – Ray and I moved to North Vancouver. His friends Ted and Jean Michel were no longer a couple. Ted opened a restaurant with his new boyfriend, but the restaurant didn't last long and a few months afterwards the boyfriend died from AIDS.

I was hired as an auxiliary correctional officer at the Vancouver Pre-Trial Services Centre, close to Vancouver's infamous skid row and Chinatown. It was a jail similar to the Edmonton Remand Centre where prisoners did time until they were either found innocent or guilty and then set free or transferred to another institution.

Joe bought "Baby" that summer, a 1968, two-door, "cocksucker red" (his words) Pontiac Parisienne with a soft top. Baby was a big, fabulous, all chrome and metal, boat of a car which Joe would eventually restore to its original splendour. Baby was Joe's pride and joy and he reveled in driving it. He loved that it screamed, "Look at me!"

One afternoon I dropped in on Joe and his friends visiting from Edmonton. When I was telling them what I was reading in the newspaper about HIV and AIDS, they dismissed me. I was a worry wart and the story was mere media hype. Sam said his boyfriend was a specialist who worked with viruses at Edmonton's University Hospital, and it was a known fact viruses could be killed. Neither Sam nor his boyfriend would make it out of the AIDS crisis alive. We just never thought that "it" would touch us the way "it" did. We never imagined "it" would become what "it" would become. Lucky for me, I was in a monogamous relationship with Ray when so many others were unknowingly being infected.

In August, I attended my first ever Gay Pride parade. Joe was in the parade along with his new buddy Paul, and both were dressed in tough, French maid drag. When Joe saw me watching from the sidelines he marched over to me, pointed at me and screamed, "I know him! I know him! And he knows me!", then laughed and walked away.

Fall, 1984 - With Ray's and my relationship ending and with Ted's boyfriend recently deceased, the timing was perfect for Ray and Ted to move to Los Angeles with hopes of eventually getting their green cards. Joe, along with his buddies Robbin and Paul formed a tough drag trio called "The Waitresses". Paul was more commonly known as Gramma, appropriately named being he was the oldest of the Waitresses trio. Their late-night show at Doll & Penny's restaurant on Davie Street became wildly popular.

Spring, 1985 - Shortly after moving to L.A., Ray and Ted quickly found refrigeration and air conditioning jobs working under the table. Ray was quick to find a love interest which made me jealous. I missed him dearly. After a few months, I decided to pay him a visit. Weeks before going, I dieted and worked out like a man on a mission. When I arrived in L.A., I looked damn hot. Ray and I had a great time hanging out for a week and fucking like mad dogs in heat. We also played tourists and went on the Space Mountain ride at Disneyland while high on magic mushrooms. What impressed me most was seeing the Bates house from the movie Psycho, on the Universal Studios tour. I had hoped Ted would accompany us on a few of our outings but he was always too exhausted. When he got home from work he went directly to bed and stayed there until the next morning. Ray said Ted was also having heavy night sweats. It didn't sound good and we suspected the worst. I was sad to leave when my week was over. Ray and I had spent an excellent time together, but it was not meant to be.

Summer, 1985 - As part of a temporary federal contract, Joe got hired on as a junior draftsman. Janice, a young woman in charge of the project required an assistant. She interviewed two candidates, Joe, and a very handsome, fit, young man. Janice said she would have loved to have hired the eye candy but knew he would be too much of a distraction and instead hired Joe, the obvious gay guy. Joe said for once being an obvious fag finally worked in his favour. Joe and Janice became fast friends and later we would all become like family. Janice loved that Joe performed in drag and when they were ahead of schedule on the job, they would often sketch and design dresses that Joe would create and wear in various drag shows and events. There was a store on Main Street with elegant dresses always on display in their window and every time we drove past Joe would point at a dress and declare, "Girl, I would look fabulous in that dress".

Baby was in the pride parade that summer and several more thereafter with the soft top down and the Waitresses, all dolled up in their tough drag fabulousness perched up on the back with their sleek legs dangling over the backseat and waving to their fans. The Waitresses became so popular they performed shows all over Vancouver, Seattle and Portland.

On July 25, the world was shocked to see Rock Hudson on TV looking very thin and unrecognizable. It was revealed he was gay and had AIDS. This would be repeated over and over between gay men and their families. "Hello, I'm gay. I have AIDS. I'm going to die." There was desperation to find a cure and gay men offered themselves as human guinea pigs. Too many of them had nothing to lose. I remember an early test some guys on the softball team submitted to and it involved getting scratched on the upper part of the arm or shoulder. Depending on the reaction it indicated whether or not they had possibly been exposed to the HIV virus. AIDS was considered a gay disease and governments were unsympathetic. They offered very little funding or support of any kind. It was politically expedient to let us die. Fighting against bigotry and for our rights and freedoms was nothing new, but fighting for our lives with urgency was. The gay community was no longer willing to lie down and continue dying. Gay men and their allies stepped out from the shadows with a fierceness, strength and intelligence that would create leaders and heroes out of many ordinary citizens.

October 2, 1985 - Rock Hudson died of AIDS confirming that no one was safe from this disease. As the number of casualties rapidly increased, all our lives, straight and gay were affected. AIDS pitted the gay man against himself, his lover, friends, family, neighbours, community and his government. It was a time when the world seemed to be against him. World culture took a hard hit; writers, actors, musicians, painters, photographers, fashion designers, models, drag queens – a wealth of talent robbed from the world. As the gay community continued to fight for their lives and to inform and educate the public at large, the province and the city of Vancouver was preoccupied with preparing for Expo '86.

Spring/Summer, 1986 - In early spring, Ted returned to Vancouver and went directly from the airport to being admitted into St. Paul's Hospital. Our worst fears were realized. Ted was very sick with AIDS. On May 2nd, Ray moved back to Vancouver, coincidentally, the same day Expo opened. Joe was advancing career wise. He began working as a draftsman for an up and coming architecture firm in the city. Even though the city was alive that summer and it was exciting to be a part of it, HIV and AIDS remained a dark cloud hanging over us.

Fall, 1986 - On September 4th, Ray's best buddy Ted died of AIDS. Ted's ex-partner Jean Michel also died around the same time. Amongst Ray's circle of friends from when we first met, Ted, Jean Michel, Dale, and his friend Joe, only Ray would survive AIDS.

I started writing again. I pulled out the stage play I had written while living in Edmonton and began converting it into a screenplay. I volunteered to work midnights at the Pre-Trial Centre and between hourly cell checks, I banged out my first screenplay titled, When Tomorrow Never Comes. When I later enrolled in a screenwriting course, I learned the length of a screenplay was between ninety and one hundred and twenty pages long. At three hundred plus pages, my screenplay was no doubt overwritten. I loved writing and this time I wouldn't stop. Writing would become my passion and becoming a writer would be my life's obsession.

One night when Joe and I were out for a steam and cruising for sex at the Club Vancouver bathhouse, Joe hooked up with Roger, a Frenchman in his late 30s. They had a fun night and later went on a few dates. But Joe liked Roger more than Roger liked Joe. Joe was not Roger's type and Roger was not Joe's type, as Joe would later come to realize. I was more Roger's type, but Roger was not my type. Roger's story was that he and a former longtime boyfriend did well for themselves running a popular clothing store, selling the latest fashions they brought back from London and Paris. Roger said anybody who was anybody visited their store. He and the boyfriend enjoyed the high life until they lost everything to a heroin addiction. In the end, Roger was selling himself for sex to pay for their drug habit. Joe and I met Roger when he was just bouncing back from the bottom.

Christmas, 1986 - Roger lived in a great character home in Burnaby and invited Joe and myself to join him and his roommate Don for Christmas dinner. Before dinner, the four of us sat about the living room having a few drinks, smoking pot and chit chatting. After a few beers on an empty stomach, combined with sitting so close to the roaring fireplace, I suddenly felt really drunk. I said nothing but knew I really needed to eat soon. Finally the turkey and ham dinner was on the table and we sat down to eat. After devouring everything on my plate, I had an urgent need to vomit. Acting like nothing was wrong I passed on having seconds, excused myself from the table and calmly made my way to the bathroom. I made it just in time. As soon as I locked the bathroom door and turned around the vomit rocketed from my gut and luckily with perfect aim flew directly into the toilet. I could not have prayed for a better shot. Disaster and embarrassment was averted. Being invited back again was now a possibility. I washed my face with cold water, rubbed toothpaste across my teeth and left the bathroom feeling like a new man. I returned to the dinner table, acted like nothing happened and changed my mind about having seconds. I could have gone for what they would have perceived as thirds, but I didn't want to come across as a glutton and chose to leave room for dessert instead. Months later when I told this story to Joe and Roger, they laughed saying they had no idea. From that Christmas on, Roger became a part of our gay family.

Spring, 1987 - Now that a blood test was available for the HIV virus leading to AIDS, Joe and I gave blood. We no longer had to wait for our health to start deteriorating before finding out that we were HIV positive. After getting tested there was an agonizing three week wait for the results. Prayers were said. Fingers were crossed. When Joe and I went back for our test results, sitting in the waiting room and waiting to see the nurse was torture. I wasn't sure if I really wanted to know. I feared that in mere moments my life could change forever and not in a good way. I feared living with a death sentence hanging over my head. Joe and I wished each other good luck. Luck was on my side. I tested negative. Joe wasn't so lucky. He was positive. Joe said being told he was HIV positive was like being hit over the head with a sledge hammer. All he wanted to do was run out of the office, but said he couldn't get his legs to move.

I felt horrible for him. There wasn't much I could say except to point out that he was still in good health and he wasn't showing any signs of the virus. Accompanying Joe's HIV diagnosis was an immediate sense of shame, guilt, fear, and depression. As could be expected Joe was devastated. He lost all interest in sex and said he couldn't even get hard to jerk off.

Summer, 1987 - Roger's roommate moved out and Ray moved in. Roger needed a roommate and Ray wanted out of the apartment he was renting. They hardly knew each other but had met on the odd occasion through Joe or myself. Months earlier, Ray and I had sex for the last time. It felt awkward and afterwards we both knew it was really over. Ray distanced himself from me and I saw him less. However, Joe and I had been hanging out at Roger's more frequently, so when Ray moved in with Roger, I began seeing more of him and we eventually rekindled our friendship. It is what we do well in our gay community, we become best friends with our exes.

The architecture firm Joe worked for started training him as a programmer for CADD software - computer-aided design and drafting. I took another screenwriting course through the New Play Centre on Granville Island. It was nine sessions over the summer called "Writing for Film through a Director's Point of View", with John Wright as the instructor. A few weeks into the course, John read my screenplay, When Tomorrow Never Comes, and liked it enough to option it with the intent to raise the money and shoot the film. I was elated to have my first screenplay optioned. The option would eventually expire, but it encouraged me to continue my pursuit of becoming a writer. I bought my first computer from John, a Kaypro word processor that used 5 and 1/4 inch floppy discs, was portable, weighed twenty-some pounds and cost me eight hundred dollars.

Joe and I moved back in together, this time sharing a large, two-bedroom suite at 19th and Cambie. Shortly after moving in we both started dating someone. Joe dated Vernon, an overall nice guy who liked Joe for the smart and interesting man that he was and seemed indifferent to Joe's dresses in the closet. I dated Doug, a talented musician and as well, an overall nice guy. This time Joe's relationship would last longer than mine. Mine turned out to be no more than, as Joe would call it, an "affairette".

Fall, 1987 - Along with six other up-and-coming Vancouver writers, I was invited to be part of the new screenwriter's unit at the New Play Centre. It was an exciting opportunity for me. I read from my new film script, Black and Blue - a drama set down home in the 1950s, about a middle-aged artist sharing her life with a closeted gay husband and an alcoholic mother. Being competitive, I wanted my screenplay to be the best of the group. As hoped for, my reading was well received and created a positive buzz. My hard work paid off. Joe wasn't a big fan of my writing. He said my scripts were too "Tennessee Williams", full of oversexed hillbillies. He meant it as an insult. I took it as a compliment. When I discovered the work of Tennessee Williams and other American Southern writers, I was hooked. I felt a kinship with their stories and characters.

Saturday, December 12, 1987 - I began another lifelong obsession – journaling my life and keeping a diary. Over the years I would accumulate a large collection of journals, mostly in notebooks, pen on paper. On this particular date I noted in my journal, "I am fat." At the time, I was not fat. I worked out in the gym five days a week, two hours a day, plus an hour of cardio and doing steroids. I also questioned on this day if moving in with Joe was the right thing to do. It had been a few months since we had moved in together and he was starting to get to me. Joe had a habit of liking to "pick", pointing out whatever he considered to be faults, no matter how minor. One habit Joe had that particularly irked me was when I got paid every second Friday and came home with a case of beer, never fail, he would comment, "Oh look. Bob has a case of beer. It must be Friday and he just got paid." Every time, never fail, and every time all I heard was my mother who had exactly the same irritating habit.

Spring, 1988 - I worked as many midnight shifts as possible at the Pre-Trial Centre. I brought my portable Kaypro computer with me and worked on my screenplays in between cell checks. I lucked out when I was assigned midnight shifts at the Vancouver General Hospital for a few months babysitting inmate Joe, a thirty-five-year-old Native man who lived on skid row. Prisoner Joe was a serious alcoholic with infectious tuberculosis. He was charged under the health act and remained in the hospital under guarded supervision until he was TB free. Years earlier, inmate Joe came to Vancouver from Whitehorse to study forestry at the University of British Columbia, but unfortunately he said he got in with the wrong crowd and all good intentions were lost to alcohol. He regretted his choices. I noted in my journal, "Hell is when you know you're living in it." During the night when prisoner Joe slept I sat in the hallway outside his room with my Kaypro computer in front of me. After a few months of babysitting inmate Joe, I had new drafts of both my screenplays: Black and Blue, and When Tomorrow Never Comes.

April 30, 1988 – I mailed a letter to my sister Cindy telling her I'm gay. I have a hard time writing that word, "GAY". One day I hope I can proudly accept it in myself. With no potential wife, nor mother for my mother's grandchildren, my mother suspects something is wrong. Not having a girlfriend has become a burden. Whether in a letter or talking with my mother or sisters on the phone, I'm constantly being asked if I have a girlfriend yet. The answer is always no. According to mother, at the ripe old age of twenty-eight I'm not getting any younger, and it was high time I started thinking about settling down and starting a family. In my letter to Cindy, I asked her to let the rest of my family in on my lifelong secret. I thought in my absence if Cindy told the family I was gay, they could absorb the information, react honestly and then individually decide if they accepted me or not. I'll accept their decisions, but either way it's time for me to move on with them in or out of my life.

May, 1988 - Cindy received my letter a few days prior to Mother's Day. As with most holidays, family gatherings and dinners were held at our parents' house. Mother's Day was no exception. Everyone was there except me. Shortly after Cindy arrived at the house on Saturday afternoon she told my mom and dad that I was gay. My mother cried and blamed herself. My father didn't care. My brother Pat was the most prejudiced until years later when his only child, a teenage daughter, outs herself as lesbian or bisexual. Considering the teasing I received growing up, I didn't understand how my being gay could be a surprise to anyone in the family. The teasing may have been fun for them, but as a young man it was torture for me. I came out to my family to stop them from asking me about having a girlfriend and getting married. It worked. From that day forward no family member would ever again ask if I found someone to love and settle down with. It seemed now that I was gay, it wasn't so important anymore. That night the family went to the Mother's Day dance at the Legion. My mother who never drinks, drank a few beers too many, and for the first and last time in her life got drunk. When my father put my mother to bed that night, she puked all over his pants. Needless to say it was a Mother's Day no one in the family would soon forget, especially my mother. A week or so later, I received a letter from my mother.

Dear Bobby:

Cindy told us about your lifestyle. We kind of had an idea but now it is fact. It hurt at first, but I told her you were our son and would accept you no matter what. I cried, got drunker than hell and only made myself sick as a dog and came up with the same conclusion that you were our son whom we love. You were always a boy any parents could be proud of. So as far as we are concerned, you are that same son. We will always love you no matter what your lifestyle is. The only thing is you should come home more often. You should come home for Christmas as you have not been home at Christmas since you went away in 1979.

Love, Mom.

Thursday, May 12, 1988 – Last night, Roger and I had a blast at Denman Station. As usual we drank, played pool, and had many good laughs. Roger and I have been hanging out a lot over the last several months and we always enjoy our time together. After leaving the bar and walking back to the car, Roger confided in me that his last HIV test came back positive. That was devastating news. It was too unexpected. I went home and cried an alcohol induced cry that ended in sobs. It was beyond sad.

Roger would later confide in me that he had actually tested positive around the same time as Joe but didn't say anything because he was scared he might have been the one who infected Joe. Joe told me to tell Roger that he had a good idea who he got "it" from and it wasn't him.

June 20, 1988 - Many senior probation and parole officers were offered early retirement and there was a need to fill the holes left behind. Correctional officers who qualified and passed the interview were offered one year seconded positions. Fortunately, my two-year Correctional Worker Diploma plus my experience in the community-based jails was good enough to secure me one of the positions. I started working at a probation office located at 8th Avenue and Manitoba Street. I would never go back to working at the Pre-Trial Services Centre again and left behind the world of men living in concrete cages with steel doors. ... Roger has a lingering cold that has us worried.

Sunday, July 3, 1988 - A hot summer day. Ray was driving up to Radium Hot Springs with his new buddies Denny and Greg who are partners. Greg's a DJ with a country music radio station and he's obsessed with his long black hair and constantly brushes it. Roger and I were invited along. The two of us went in Roger's car. Poor Roger, it wasn't a good day for him. He was easily winded after a short walk. The poor guy is thin and fearing for his life. He said he enjoys spending time with me because I put him in a good mood.

End of July, 1988 - Roger was looking somewhat frail but feeling better. His friend Bradley visited from San Francisco and it didn't go well. Roger said Bradley was dying from AIDS but wouldn't admit to having it, deal with it, face it, or talk about it. Roger said it was very hard on him.

A week before Roger's fortieth birthday, I bought him a pre-birthday gift, a coffee cup with "OLD FART" written repeatedly across the cup. Roger didn't think it was funny but eventually accepted the cup with good humour and placed it on the top shelf in the kitchen cupboard. One day, Roger noticed the cup was missing. He questioned Ray and Ray pleaded ignorance, but in fact Ray had broken the cup by accident. Days later, Roger noticed the cup was back on the top shelf. Ray had found an identical cup, said nothing and replaced it. Neither Roger nor Ray commented on its reappearance, but I heard all about it.

On August 4th, Joe, Ray, Roger and I celebrated Roger's fortieth birthday at Nick's Spaghetti House on Commercial Drive. I gave Roger a water gun, a jigsaw puzzle, a yo-yo, and a stuffed Garfield cat with suction cups. Roger loved them all. The Garfield cat became a permanent fixture on his rear passenger car window.

I was tested again for HIV and did a lot of bargaining. I didn't want to live with that death sentence over my head. I didn't want to live with that day to day worry that my next cold could be the end of me. I didn't want to slowly waste away to nothing. When the three weeks were up, I returned to my doctor's office for the results. Sitting in the waiting room, the walk to the doctor's office, watching the doctor open my file and finally reading the results was excruciating. For a moment, I couldn't breathe. I finally could relax when I was told I was still HIV negative. Joe remained in good health, but I couldn't say the same for Roger.

Every two weeks when our biweekly newspaper Xtra West came out, the "Proud Lives" section was the go-to page to see who had recently died of AIDS. Every two weeks there was a page or two of fresh faces and our responses were the same - "Oh no, not him too,"

... "Oh no, not her too." Shock, surprise, sorrow and grief hit us with each issue.

Joe got word from Edmonton that his former roommate and best friend Sam was now sick with AIDS. Joe says not a day goes by where he does not think about himself being HIV positive.

Friday, August 19, 1988 - Joe worked earlier in the day installing CADD software for a local drafting firm. When he arrived home around noon, we loaded our suitcases and camping gear into the car and took Baby on a road trip - destination, two weeks in Guerneville, California, aka Russian River, a small-town gay Mecca located an hour and a half north of San Francisco. My only concern was leaving Roger behind. His cold came back and knocked the wind out of him.

As we approached Seattle, a sense of horror came over Joe. Before leaving the office he worked at in the morning, he used one of their computers to email Janice a letter telling her about an upcoming Coronation Ball and the fabulous new gown he was planning to wear. He then left the office, forgetting to delete the letter. Joe feared someone finding the letter on their computer but with us nearing Seattle it was too late to turn back. Another work-related gay faux pas Joe confessed to was when a female co-worker asked Joe what size shoes he wore and without thinking he just blurted out, "Men's or women's?" Joe said he couldn't stop the words from racing out of his mouth. The co-worker looked momentarily confused which provided Joe with the opportunity to make a joke out of it.

When we arrived in Seattle we picked up an ounce of pot from a friend of Joe's and continued on our way. We drove for two days; smoking pot, talking, listening to music and laughing. We discussed our past, our future, our dreams, our doubts, our wants and needs. Of course, the dark cloud of AIDS hung over us. It was late, around 11 PM when we checked into The Willows camp grounds in Russian River and pitched our tent in the dark. Early the next morning we awoke to the sound of ducks close by. When we opened the tent flaps and looked outside, we had pitched our tent right next to the ducks pen. After moving the tent, Joe and I hung out for the week smoking pot, reading, writing, exploring the area and letting the days drift by. For a small town there certainly was a lot of gay - bars, guest houses, gym and camp grounds. I was impressed to find out such a place existed. As planned, we headed into San Francisco to party for the weekend. Before leaving we packed what we were taking with us into the trunk of the car. The next thing I see, Joe's unpacking everything and frantically searching for his wallet. The longer Joe searched the more frustrated he became, and I was his number one suspect. He had reason to suspect me. The previous day we bought food for supper and when it was time to eat we couldn't find the groceries. I eventually found the groceries in the garbage can. I had cleaned up around the tent and in my stoned state I'd thrown the groceries out. What frustrated and upset Joe more than the loss of his credit cards and driver's license was the loss of our party drugs. There were two hits of acid inside his wallet.

Before leaving for the two hour drive, we ate lunch at a local restaurant. When it came time to pay I pulled my money out of my pocket and along with my money was Joe's driver's license. Why I was in possession of Joe's driver's license is still a mystery to me. To Joe, it was overwhelming proof that I was responsible for his missing wallet and even more so the missing hits of acid.

San Francisco was much cooler than what we'd experienced over the previous few days. Joe had a friend who was out of the city for the weekend and he let us crash at his place. That evening before heading out, we decided it was cool enough to be wearing jackets. I was standing in the bathroom brushing my teeth when I heard a loud shriek coming from the living room, "Bob!" Joe shrieked, "Guess what?"

"You found it," I called back, meaning his wallet.

"Yes," Joe said, "I found the acid!" I was vindicated. Joe's wallet had fallen out of his inside jacket pocket, slipped down the sleeve and got lodged in the cuff. I was suddenly off the hook. We dropped the acid, went out to the bars and had a great time hanging out and cruising men. Normally we would have gone to the baths while coming down from the acid, but they were closed down due to the AIDS crisis. Late Sunday morning we drove north and returned to the camp grounds. We hung out for the remainder of the week relaxing and enjoying each other's company.

The camp grounds were adjacent to the river and one hot afternoon I decided to smoke a bit of pot, slather on some sun screen, grab the inflatable raft and go hang out on the river. A prissy queen sitting by the riverbank and smoking a cigarette completely ignored me as I waded knee deep into the water. Being careful to not have the sunscreen wash off me, I placed the rubber raft on the water, held it in place, and took a giant leap forward aiming for the centre of the raft. As soon as my greased up body hit the rubber, the raft flew in one direction and my body in the other. As soon as I hit the water I knew my mistake. I busted out laughing uncontrollably over my stupidity. I swallowed water, started choking and couldn't stop laughing. I could have easily drowned if I hadn't gotten out of the water. Throughout, the prissy queen on the riverbank didn't crack a smile. He finished his cigarette and acted like nothing happened.

At the end of our second week we drove back to Vancouver, contemplating life along the way. Over the following days and weeks, Joe would come up to me from out of nowhere and yell, "Hey Bob, guess what?" And I'd yell back, "You found the acid!" And we'd laugh.

September/October, 1988 – I'm spending weekends at the house with Roger. His cold is still hanging on. He isn't looking good and he's lost weight. While he lies on the couch in the living room sleeping in front of the fireplace, I sit at the table on the back porch, smoking pot and pecking away at the keyboard on my computer. I'm always writing. Roger's doctor has decided it's time for Roger to start taking AZT, but he has to wait eight weeks before the pills become available. In the meantime, Roger's health continues to worsen.

I moved again. Joe finally got to me. I didn't move out because I was mad at Joe and I still wanted to be his friend. I moved out because I didn't come all the way out west to end up living with my mother. I was done with his picking and unnecessary comments. I moved into a one-bedroom suite in an apartment building not far from where Joe and I initially moved into, across from the Mount Pleasant Community Centre. Joe moved only three blocks away. His apartment was much nicer than mine with a large balcony facing the North Shore Mountains and a view that spanned from the West End to east Vancouver. Joe was peeved at me for moving out on him, but with my apartment having green shag carpet, matching curtains and a back alley view, it was easier for him to forgive me. But then he'd always been more concerned with being part of the ten percent of the ten percent crowd than I was.

Joe received bad news about his friend and fellow Waitress partner Paul, aka Gramma. Joe said Paul's white cell blood count was way down and he too has to start taking AZT.

I started working out at Gold's Gym and convinced Joe to join as well. He called it the big boy's gym and was intimidated at first but relaxed once he realized no one cared if he was queer. One day I arrived at the gym after Joe and watched him knocking off a serious set of reps on the leg press. I chuckled to myself knowing Joe wasn't much into leg exercises. I had a suspicion of what was going on, so I went up to him, leaned in close, and casually asked if he was planning on wearing a dress soon. Joe laughed. He said I knew him all too well. Indeed, there was an upcoming ball and he was determined to be sporting some hot gams in his heels and fabulous new dress.

November, 1988 - Roger's eight week waiting period for the AZT pills was up and he had not heard back from his doctor. On Thursday before the Remembrance Day long weekend, I phoned Roger's doctor. There was no answer so I left a message asking him to call me back regarding Roger's AZT pills. By the end of the day he had not returned my call. The following morning after arriving at the probation office, I called again. This time I spoke with the doctor's receptionist. She apologized for Rogers's doctor not getting back to me and said the doctor had already left for the long weekend. I informed her of how sick Roger was and stressed his need for the medication. She apologized again and told me to call back after the long weekend. I remained calm but assertive. I asked her if she could tell me if Roger's AZT pills were in, but she told me she could not disclose that information. I again stressed to her how sick Roger was. The receptionist told me that she sympathized but again insisted that she could not disclose the information. I remained insistent. The receptionist held her ground but finally divulged Roger's AZT pills were in, but I couldn't get them from her. I'd need to go through the pharmacist at St. Paul's Hospital. I thanked the receptionist for her time and generosity and immediately called the pharmacist at St. Paul's Hospital. Like the receptionist, the pharmacist said she could not disclose any information to me. I told her all I needed to know was whether or not Roger's AZT pills were there. We went through the same loop;

no, she couldn't tell me. I remained polite but assertive knowing if I crossed the slightest line she could end our conversation at any time. Eventually, she disclosed that Roger's AZT pills were there. Now I needed to know how to get them. She informed me she was the only pharmacist in the city dispensing the medication and Roger would have to make an appointment to see her. However, she was booked solid and it would take several weeks if not months for Roger to get an appointment. That was not good enough. Still polite, I threatened to go to the media if Roger had to wait that long for his possibly lifesaving meds. I explained he was lying on the couch, dying. By the time my conversation ended with the pharmacist, Roger had an appointment to see her on the following Wednesday. If Roger missed his appointment, she said he would go to the bottom of the list. She then directed me to the hospital's social worker who provided information about an organization called People with AIDS (PWA). Through PWA, I was able to connect with a guy who lived in the West End and was collecting AZT from those whose bodies were rejecting the medication, so people like Roger could begin taking AZT while waiting for access to their prescription. Free of charge the guy supplied me with enough AZT pills to get Roger started along with instructions on how the pills should be taken. There was a strict regime and it required Roger to set his alarm clock so he could wake up in the middle of the night and take his pills. Because the Vander Zalm government refused to pay for the AZT medication, the guy said to toss any request for payment into the garbage.

The following Wednesday when Roger finally saw the pharmacist, she told him she had never before spoken with anyone who could be so polite yet so rude in all the same tone. At first, the AZT pills worked for Roger. He gained weight. He looked healthier. He was finally able to get off the couch and was more than happy to send me packing. He was done listening to the clack, clack, clack of me pounding away at my keyboard. I was happy my good buddy Roger was up and feeling alive again. His spirits picked up considerably and he was able to go back to work. He claimed I saved his life. I did nothing different than what others were doing for their friends and lovers throughout our gay communities. Roger told me he had a needle full of heroin in his night table drawer and when his time comes his death would be from a heroin overdose. He said it was the perfect way to go. He also told me that he wanted his ashes spread across the dance floor at the Gandydancer in memory of all the good times he's had there. As a young man, Roger left home and his family in Montreal because he was gay. Being raised a strict Catholic, he said they'd never approve. So he hitchhiked across the country, landed in Vancouver, came out, and never saw his family again. On occasions when reminiscing, Roger would get out a photo album and show me photos of his family. He loved and missed his mother the most. Once feeling better, Roger and Ray took a trip home to Montreal. Ray went to visit the aunt who raised him and Roger hoped to reconnect with his family for what he knew would be his last time. Ray went with Roger to the family home Roger had grown up in and took photos of Roger standing on the front porch. Roger didn't have it in him to face his family. He felt too ashamed. He didn't have it in him to tell his family that he was gay and dying of AIDS. Roger returned to Vancouver without seeing his family ever again.

December, 1988 – Not long after coming back from Montreal, Ray and Roger had a major disagreement and Ray moved out. Roger got mad at me for not siding with him but I refused to take sides. Their argument ended our social gatherings at the house and our good times together as one big happy gay family. Roger isolated himself and refused to see us. He reunited with his former partner and his friend Don moved back into the house.

Spring, 1989 - In March, Joe's old roommate and best friend Sam arrived from Edmonton for the Coronation Ball. By now Sam had full-blown AIDS and we were warned he didn't look healthy and to be prepared for a shock. We visited at the hotel where Sam was staying and it was both shocking and disheartening to see him. Sam was in drag and beneath the thick pancake makeup covering his puffy face I could see large purple spots. This was my first time seeing Kaposi's sarcoma lesions. In another month, Sam would decide to stop taking all medications and accept his impending death. As much as he wanted to live there was no hope. Joe went back to Edmonton to visit for one last time and on April 27, Sam died from AIDS. He was in his late twenties. His Marlene Dietrich would be no more.

I ran into Ray's friends Denny and Greg. I wasn't prepared to see Greg looking so thin and gaunt. He too would soon lose his battle against AIDS.

One Saturday night at Celebrities Nightclub, I met Ben. We had a few dates, but a relationship was not in our cards. He would though replace Roger as my drinking and pool playing buddy and become family. A few weeks after knowing Ben, he confided in me that he was HIV positive and convinced that he would never reach his thirty-fifth birthday.

Summer, 1989 - On a Sunday afternoon when I was playing softball at the Brockton Oval ball field, Roger's roommate Don showed up to tell me Roger tried to commit suicide and was taken away by ambulance. Don said it was more of a cry for help than a serious attempt. I wanted to visit but Roger refused to see me.

In August, I went home to visit my family for the second time since coming out. My being gay was now widely known within the family. A day or so after being home, my mother phoned a family friend to ask if she could sub for her on the women's bowling team. The friend wasn't available, but said perhaps my mother could ask me to sub. Her offence was mild in comparison to what I experienced a few days later when visiting my sister. Coincidentally, my uncle, another one of my mother's brothers, was visiting his in-laws next door. When my uncle saw me, he verbally let loose and made sure that he was loud enough for everyone in the vicinity to hear. He yelled that I was a disgusting, fucking faggot and queer and that I should go back to Vancouver and not be spreading my AIDS around town. I froze. I was too shocked and humiliated to respond. It was a horrific and disgusting attack. It was also demoralizing being ridiculed in front of my family. No one in my family said anything except for some quiet grumbling, and we all moved on like nothing happened.

Spring, 1990 - Ray is feeling blue. His new boyfriend Leroy, who is only in his young twenties is HIV positive. As for Joe, he has a yeast infection inside his mouth called thrush. How can he think it's not AIDS related? There's no feeling healthy or safe once you've tested positive.

A group of us went to see the film Longtime Companion. It's the first Hollywood film to deal with the AIDS crisis and its effect on the gay community. Amongst the ten of us who went to the film, only three are not HIV positive. Of those who are, some are doing better than others. All we can do is hope a cure is soon on the way. We are tired of watching our friends die off. All levels of government continue to drag their heels on this AIDS crisis and are fine with just letting us die. They need to stop seeing this as a gay disease. The gay community is united and continues to fight. "SILENCE = DEATH" and "PLAY SAFE" are the signs of our time. Right now condoms and education are the only protection we have against this virus.

August 4 to 11, 1990 - The Vancouver Gay Games took place with the opening and closing ceremonies at BC Place

Stadium. There was a lot of opposition. The Fraser Valley church members took out full-page ads in The Vancouver Sun and The Province condemning the event as proof of an "impending sodomite invasion" and encouraged residents to pray against the event. Joe was annoyed with me for not going to watch the games. He said it was a once in a lifetime opportunity. Except for playing softball, I've never been much of a sports fan. He was also miffed at me for refusing to drive Baby in the pride parade. The plan was for the Waitresses to be sprawled across the back of Baby and holding up a sign, "THE WAITRESSES WELCOME THE WORLD". I was still too closeted at work to do that.

October 26, 1990 - My dear friend Roger died of AIDS. A few days before his death, Roger's roommate Don called to say Roger was hospitalized in the palliative care ward. I asked if he'd ask Roger if I could visit. Roger agreed. Our first visit was awkward. What to say? Where to start? He was sick but cognizant. I didn't stay long, but the ice was broken. I returned two days later around supper time. Roger was now in a private room. We were alone. We reminisced and laughed about old times. He was in good spirits. I fed him his supper and he ate voraciously, like he had not eaten in some time. As soon as he finished eating he puked up everything. I cleaned him up. He apologized. Then he wanted a cigarette. I asked the nurse if Roger could have a cigarette and the nurse looked at me like I was crazy. When I left, I gave Roger a big hug and told him I'd be back the following day. I left happy with the feeling that the old Roger was back and we were good again. Shortly after returning home, I received a phone call. Roger had passed away. I was taken by total surprise. It didn't make sense. I had just been with him. He seemed quite okay to me. What I didn't know at the time was Roger's death was imminent. If I had known I would have stayed and kept him company. He died alone. What I do know for sure is for the last few years of Roger's life, when Joe, myself, and Ray were it, Roger's life was filled with friendship, warmth, celebration, love, and lots of laughter. During our last summer together, Roger and I had our routine. After supper we would start out with an ice cream cone from Baskin-Robbins on the corner of Davie and Denman, then walk along the seawall to Second Beach, cut through the park and end up at the Denman Station where we'd spend the next few hours drinking, playing pool, and having a good laugh. We did this a few nights during the week. Roger was one of the nicest men I've ever known and I will always treasure the few years we hung out together. He had a kind heart and he was a great pal. I'm fortunate to have known him. Joe jokingly blamed me for Roger's death, saying that I had partied him to death and when it was his time to kick the bucket, I was to keep my distance. We had a lovely service for Roger. People from his work showed up. Roger was not out to his co-workers and they were surprised to find out he was gay. After the service we all went to a pub, drank beers in Roger's honour and celebrated his life. My biggest regret was not fighting hard enough to get back into Roger's life a whole lot earlier.

December, 1990 - Christmas was fun and lighthearted this year. Joe invited seven of us for dinner at what he calls his "fab-u-lous Hollywood apartment". Dinner, the usual fare, was perfect. Pictures were taken, pot was smoked, booze was drunk, and after dinner we settled down to play the word game "Slang Teasers". Of course, the more pot smoked and booze consumed, the funnier the game became. A good time was had by all. Two days later, Joe flew to Palm Springs for New Years.

January 23, 1991 - Joe found out he has Pneumocystis Pneumonia (PCP). I felt sick inside to hear that and felt badly for him. On Sunday, I will go to church and light a candle. Joe has to go into the hospital tomorrow and have a camera inserted into his lungs. His white cell count is very low and if it doesn't improve, he will have to go on AZT. He's scared. He hurts and is a little freaked out. I can't imagine Joe being gone. I called him tonight from work and made him laugh. That's one thing we do a lot – laugh. We talked and I tried to ease his fears. I promised him I will be there when he needs me. I will continue to pray. He's terrified that he might have full-blown AIDS and have to go on AZT. He said his sleeping is erratic and he has awful dreams when he does sleep.

May, 1991 - Joe has left the drafting firm and he's now working three part-time jobs: teaching CAD Drafting part-time at BCIT, independently contracting to various architecture firms and working part-time as a waiter at Earl's On Top. He's doing very well for himself career wise and making good money. He might make it into the ten percent of the ten percent crowd after all. He recently purchased a new sofa, TV, VCR, desk, computer, carpet and prints for his fab-u-lous Hollywood apartment. He called it retail therapy. He said if he was dying sooner rather than later, he was going to enjoy what might be the last summer of his life. When we were at St. Paul's hospital yesterday, we saw the owner of The Neighbourhood Gym. He was in a wheelchair, looking sickly and like he had AIDS. At first Joe and I debated if it was actually him. For his sake, we hoped it wasn't, but I was sure it was. We were thrown for a loop seeing him. For Joe, perhaps it was a mirror of what's to come. Joe said he wants to be buried here because Vancouver is home.

Joe, I, and Gramma (Paul) saw the movie, Soapdish. It was up both of their alleys. Joe especially loved it when Cathy Moriarty's character turned out to be a sex-change. Poor Gramma looked sickly and thin. Very sad.

August 10, 1991 - Joe came back from a road trip with Baby. He went to the Coronation Ball in Edmonton and then continued home for a family reunion. He won best command performance at the ball. He drove all the way to Edmonton with the top down on Baby and arrived with a great tan. He said he looked fabulous and must have changed outfits at least seven times. Miss Jodie Jean was a star that night. On his way home to the reunion, he stopped in to see an old friend of the family. This woman knew his mother and father before the stepfather came into the picture. Joe wanted to learn more about his birth father and family history. He said he wasn't sure if he had the right house at first, but once the woman opened the door and he saw her, he knew he was at the right place. Joe said the woman had an odd habit of looking at him like she had something to say and then look away, then look back at him and tell him what she had to say. They talked about his father being an alcoholic. Aside from his alcoholism, she said Joe's father was not a bad man. She gave Joe a letter his father had written to her when he was in the hospital and dying of cancer. The father wrote about having throat cancer, being in a lot of pain, and having most of his mouth removed on the inside. Joe passed the letter on to his sister and brother. Before arriving home, Joe's mother told his stepfather that Joe was gay. His stepfather said nothing but acknowledged it. Joe said the whole trip was an emotional roller coaster.

August 20, 1991 - Joe and I had planned to go to the gym but we smoked pot and hung out at his place instead. He was depressed. He's been down about a lot of things lately and he was still thinking about his trip home and how that affected him. He received a letter from his aunt, his father's sister. After he visited the woman who gave him his father's letter, she contacted his aunt and told her about Joe. The aunt in turn wrote Joe filling him in about his father and her fond memories of him. She enclosed his mother and father's wedding photo. She wrote that she and her two brothers had a great relationship. The other brother died two years before Joe's father and afterwards is when Joe's father started drinking heavily. According to his aunt, Joe's father was a kind man, a Jack-of-all-trades and would do anything for anyone. Joe said once his mother married the stepfather whom he'd always disliked, he and his sister and brother were kept away from his father's side of the family. Joe wonders if it's because his life is coming to an end that he's receiving these insights. In between the seriousness, we managed to joke and laugh. He said it's telling as to what kind of person I am to have him as a best friend.

November 1, 1991 – Joe called to wish me a happy thirty-second birthday and to tell me that Gramma (Paul) had died overnight. This is very sad. Poor Gramma. Joe said he made a point of being there when Gramma died so that he could see what dying looked like. It wasn't as scary as he had imagined.

November 7, 1991 - Joe's friend Mickey told us that his partner of eighteen years was dying from AIDS. Mickey is praying that his partner lives through this Christmas. AIDS! It just doesn't stop. So, so many are dying.

Joe met a black guy also named Joe when he was in Seattle several weeks ago. Seattle Joe is also HIV positive.

November 9, 1991 - Joe turned thirty-three today. Seattle Joe is in Vancouver this weekend to spend time with him. The two Joes like each other, but both are at the point where their health is becoming seriously compromised. Joe says that kills his last hope for love. We went for dinner and afterwards to Denman Station for a few drinks and a few games of pool. It was a great night for everyone.

Mid-November, 1991 - Joe saw his doctor and was told his pneumonia may be back. A few days later I drove Joe to the hospital and returned twelve hours later to pick him up. He's now part of a study group for some kind of new AIDS drug. Joe said he's going to die anyway so he has nothing to lose. I pray that the new AIDS drug works miracles.

Late January, 1992 - Joe received more bad news. His helper cells are down to almost nothing. His eyes were red from crying. He asked his doctor if it's only a matter of time and his doctor said yes. Joe appreciated the honesty. I didn't know what to say except for sorry. It seems all we say is sorry these days. Joe said there's nothing to say. We both agreed that this was all just too fucking wild. I told him I'm scared to get tested. I think I'd rather not know. If I came back positive, I'd be a basket case and it would not be pretty. Joe asked, what makes me think he's not feeling that way? I told him he didn't show it. He said that's so him, good at covering up things.

Ray is concerned about his boyfriend Leroy. He got sick and had to be hospitalized, but they said it has nothing to do with AIDS. I find that hard to believe.

February, 1992 - Joe's friend Mickey lost his partner of eighteen years to AIDS. Comforting to know they were able to have one last Christmas together. Joe had ringing in his ears and wondered what he should he bracing himself for now. Turned out it was only wax build up. It was a relief, but he was prepared for the worst.

I went for an AIDS test and now I have to sweat it out for the next three weeks before I get the results. It shouldn't be positive. I haven't had unsafe sex. But then, one can never be too safe. Please God don't let me be positive. I'm not sure I want to go back and find out the results.

Joe's back in the dumps. He told me about a memory he recently had. It's from when he was young. He and his mom were sitting in the basement of his parents' house sprouting potatoes. He remembered telling her he had a feeling that he would die young by some horrible means or disease. He said he's scared shitless. But he's excited about Vancouver's Coronation Ball coming up. His plan is to do glam drag first and then later in the night do the Swedish stewardesses with two Edmonton friends, Mrs. K. and Ross. The Swedish stewardesses are hilarious. Everything is a "yoke!"

March, 1992 - I got the results from my AIDS test. I prayed to God all the way from home to the doctor's office. By the time I saw the doctor my stomach was in knots. The results were negative. I do not have HIV. When I told Ben I was still negative, he told me to hold on to it. I would hear this again from others who were HIV positive - hold on to your negative status.

Ray went to Hawaii with his friend Michael, a young man he dated off and on before meeting Leroy. While in Hawaii, Michael became sick and had to be hospitalized. Apparently he's not doing very well. It's AIDS.

Joe called. He's down to four helper cells which he has now named Eeny, Meeny, Miny, and Moe. Humour is the best and unfortunately only medicine. Joe said he had a wonderful time at the Coronation Ball. All went according to plan. He wore glamour drag during the first half of the night, followed by the Swedish stewardesses.

Joe thinks he has approximately six months to live. He told me that someone who was in the experimental drug trial with him had died. He has thrush in his mouth all the time now and he's had the shits for the last week. He can't keep anything in. Everything passes through him like water. He remains worried. He was frustrated today. He had wanted to go out and let loose last night but he can't be two feet away from a toilet.

April 15, 1992 - Around 9:10 this morning I got a phone call from The Canadian Film Centre telling me I was accepted into the Writer's Residency Program. Yahoo! Too exciting! Working towards the dream of one day getting a film made. I have to be there for the first of June. I first applied to the centre in 1989 but was rejected. I worked hard over the following three years determined to improve my credentials. I was twice accepted as a Fellow into the Praxis Screenwriting Program, had both of my screenplays optioned, and I had the support of Norm Jewison's office.

Easter Monday, April 20, 1992 - The live broadcast of The Freddie Mercury Tribute Concert for AIDS Awareness was filled with top name musicians - Elton John, George Michael, Liza Minnelli, Annie Lennox, David Bowie, and others. What a great show. Elizabeth Taylor said the same number of people who attended the concert, which was estimated at seventy-two thousand, would be infected with HIV in the next two weeks. Hard to believe that could be possible, but true.

May 1, 1992 - Joe went to Seattle this past weekend. He said it wasn't much fun. After one month he still "has the shits", as he calls it, and he's lost thirteen pounds. He's not looking healthy. He complained about his friends wanting to cry on his shoulder about the drama in their lives, while he has enough of his own to deal with. According to Joe, I'm the only friend who talks openly about his illnesses and what he's going through. We do talk often about the condition his condition is in. I feel it's healthy for him to get it out of his head now and then. The time I spent with Roger when he was getting sick has prepared me for Joe. I wonder how Joe truly feels about me moving to Toronto and going to the Canadian Film Centre. He graciously said he was happy for me. But how could he be? My life and dreams are taking off, while everything he's worked hard to achieve is coming to an end.

May 14, 1992 - Joe is aware of his weight loss. He doesn't want to go into the West End and have the queens see him. He thinks they would gossip about him having "it". The doctors tell him they can't find out why he's shitting all the time, but it's not normal. Everything passes through him. We are going to see a preview of Sister Act on Saturday night. Joe can use a laugh. He's teaching at BCIT all week.

May 18, 1992 - It's getting closer to the time for me to leave for Toronto and the Canadian Film Centre. I'm excited but scared and questioning my ability. All I can do is give it my best shot.

May 23, 1992 - A farewell bar-b-q was held in my honour at Ray's place on the weekend. There was Joe, Dale (Miss Tuesday Night), Ray, Leroy, myself, Mickey, Ben, and Tania who has moved from Edmonton and now permanently living here. It was a fun evening. Joe gave me an ounce of pot and a cheque for five hundred dollars. He said it was my inheritance from him. I'm very lucky to have and be loved by my friends. Leroy's coming along for the ride to Toronto. He plans on visiting with friends for a week or so.

May 28, 1992 - Four days after leaving Vancouver, Leroy and I arrived in Toronto. He was good company and made the trip all that more entertaining. From Calgary to Toronto was all new scenery for me. I particularly loved driving through the prairies and the vast openness. It was a long drive through Ontario to get to Toronto, but we arrived safely. Leroy is staying with his friends and

I'm sharing a two-bedroom apartment with a former college classmate who I remained friends with.

June 10, 1992 - Joe phoned from Vancouver last night and sounded depressed. He's thinking about quitting his dream job teaching at BCIT. I joked how lucky he was to be able to retire at the early age of thirty-three. He said his students stare at him. He's now lost twenty-eight pounds and his suits just hang off him. He still has the shits and he was up shitting seven times the night before. He's awaiting test results from stool samples and prays they have answers for him. It was great talking to Joe and hearing his voice. After our conversation I went to bed and had an awful dream about him dying in the hospital. He looked so sad and sick. When I woke up, I cried and cried.

June 14, 1992 - Joe phoned to let me know he might have to go into the hospital. He's down to one hundred and thirty-three pounds and can't stop shitting. I tried encouraging him to keep a positive mind.

June 21, 1992 - I wrote to Joe telling him I went to the bathhouse and finally had an orgasm with someone other than myself. I joked I almost forgot what dick tasted like and that it tasted a little like chicken. Instead of me choking the chicken, this time the chicken choked me. I'm sure he'll get a laugh out of that.

June 25, 1992 - Joe called to say hi. His mom and stepfather will be coming out to visit for a week. He wants everything in order before he dies. That's so Joe, always very sensible and orderly. He said he's scared of dying and furious at having to die at such a young age.

July 7, 1992 - Joe's family is still visiting and it's going better than expected. He's relieved to have their support. They want him to come home to die, but he told them he'll live out his life in Vancouver. He said when they go home on Thursday he'll book himself into St. Paul's hospital. He's on some new drugs and not shitting as much.

September 9, 1992 - Joe and Ray arrived for a visit. They were in Montreal first, Ray to visit his aunt, and Joe to visit his former Waitress buddy, Robbin. We had five good days of hanging out, drinking, eating, watching TV, and going to the movies. We had an overall fun time and it was great spending time with them both. Joe's thinner and doesn't look healthy. AIDS is a horrible fucking disease. I was sorry to see them go. Now I have to focus on my work at the film centre.

November 1, 1992 - I turned thirty-three today. In another eight days, Joe will be thirty-four.

January 2, 1993 - Ray paid for my flight out to Vancouver and I landed in time to celebrate New Year's Eve. The next day, he flew to Hawaii for three weeks. I'm house sitting the animals. Joe told Ray about Leroy's excessive drug use and partying. Ray got mad at Leroy and in turn Leroy got mad at Joe. Joe said he doesn't care.

Joe went home for Christmas and returned for New Year's. He said his trip home was okay. His family was very supportive and willing to help if needed. His brother-in-law though wouldn't allow Joe to visit his sister at their house because of him being HIV positive. When the sister came to the parent's house the husband stayed outside. That really bothered Joe. What a horrible and ignorant man to put Joe through such humiliation. In his bedroom at night, Joe said he would smoke pot and blow the smoke out the bedroom window. He suspects his mother and stepfather knew but didn't mention it. One night while lying in bed and being really high, Joe said he got lost in his imagination and envisioned himself on stage in full drag and belting out Whitney Houston's, "I Will Always Love You". The crowd was made up of his family and friends and he said everyone was in awe of his beauty and talent. They were crying. He was crying. Everyone was crying. He joked it was the best damn pity party he took himself on in a long time.

Joe has always been easily angered, but now he has even less patience. One has to tread carefully at times. He's so thin and doesn't look good. There are warts on his face and he still has the shits – for nine months non-stop. He said he goes to the washroom at least three times a night. He can't find clothes that fit anymore.

He said he could ignore his weight loss until he saw photos of himself and how skinny he actually was. He's scared as hell.

January 13, 1993 - Last night, Joe and I sat around chatting as we often do about the condition his condition is in. He doesn't want to drag out the inevitable. He intends to speed things along when his time nears. He doesn't want his friends watching him fade away and he wants to die at home in his fab-u-lous Hollywood apartment which represents everything he's achieved. He finds it hard to think he had such a bright future ahead of him and now it's been taken away. The whole thing's so upsetting. Joe said being with Gramma when he died has given him strength for what's to come. He said it's easier now that he's made peace with what he's going through and is as prepared as he can possibly be. At the same time, he's petrified and cries a lot when he's alone. He wants to be remembered by his friends as being brave and having done the whole dying thing with grace. When he dies, he wants half his ashes to go home with his mom and the other half spread out into English Bay. I asked Joe if he had found peace with his stepfather. He was nasty to Joe when Joe was a young sissy growing up on the farm. He said he has made some peace with the old man. He's supposed to go for lunch tomorrow with his aunt and uncle. This is his father's sister, the aunt who had written to him, but he doesn't want to go. He thinks it will be too awkward because of the "AIDS and dying thing".

January 14, 1993 - Joe went for lunch with his aunt and uncle today. He's glad he did. It went better than expected. He said his aunt took his photo three times and surprised him with giving him his father's wallet. When he got home and opened the wallet, inside was a photo of him with his sister and brother taken when they were quite young. In the change purse was his father's wedding ring. Joe said more ghosts from his past. His father died young and Joe sees his dying young as history repeating itself. He asked me if that all sounded too weird. No. I understood completely.

January 15, 1993 - I went for a few beers last night and ran into someone I have always known as "Asshole." I met "Asshole" years back when he was first coming out. He was very closeted and when I asked what his name was, he didn't want to tell me so he said call me "Asshole". So he's been known as "Asshole" ever since. Tonight when I ran into him, he was really drunk and sad and told me that he recently tested positive. I felt badly for him and gave him a big hug.

February 20, 1993 - I'm back in Toronto and back at the film centre. We are all focused on our final project, the making of our short films. Joe called. He said he went to the Coronation Ball in Seattle and had a great time. He said his health is the same. Joe was vain about his looks so his obvious change in appearance must be hard on him. He told me about all these guys who have died recently. This AIDS tsunami does not stop.

February 23, 1993 - There was a story in the news about a new AIDS treatment, requiring three pills to be taken at once. I pray to God that this is the cure. Poor Joe is not on any medication. They want him to try a new one and they are very expensive.

March 29, 1993 - They have found the answer to Joe's shitting problem. According to the doctor not many people have been infected with this and they are now learning how to manage it. Identifying the problem has given Joe some relief. He went out for brunch with Leroy and Ray on Sunday. I miss them. I wished I was there to go with them. Joe said he missed me and it's not the same without me there.

April 17, 1993 - Joe called tonight. He's in a lot of pain and has a problem with his bladder. When he has a bowel movement he's in pain for at least ten minutes and it hurts all the way to the head of his penis. Ouch! He has plans to go home in July to see his sister's new baby. I asked him if her husband would allow that. He said if not, he will never go home again. In August he's going to the Edmonton Ball and that will be his last command performance.

May 10, 1993 - I got a card in the mail from Ben. Inside was a bit of pot and a hit of acid. It was great to hear from him. I'm finished at the film centre. The short film I wrote has been shot and is now in the hands of the director and editor.

May 26, 1993 - I will soon start working part-time as a correctional officer at a halfway house run by the Salvation Army. Ray called to say Joe's not doing well. He's down to one hundred and ten pounds. Sadly, he's in his final week working at BCIT. Joe said he held on at work for as long as he could, but it's now over.

June 14, 1993 - Joe called. He sounded awful. He said he felt shitty, had no appetite, and was exhausted by his mother's visit. She was constantly asking if she could get him anything. Poor woman. I'm sure he was short with her at times. It must be horribly difficult for her to go through this. She wanted to take Joe home but he said no. He would just go there and wait to die, whereas in Vancouver he can be around friends who can relate to what he's going through. I need to get there sooner rather than later. First Roger and now it's Joe. Every time I think of Roger, I smile and chuckle to myself. He was a good man and a great friend.

I spoke with Ray and he said Joe's not looking at all well. Also, Leroy's health is becoming compromised and he's having problems with his legs and feet.

June 16, 1993 - I called Joe's friend Mickey and he told me he'd be surprised if Joe lasts much longer. Mickey warned me to be prepared for when I see Joe as he's incredibly skinny and gaunt. I called Joe and told him I was coming out. He said there is no need to rush. I have a suspicion he doesn't want me seeing him looking the way he is.

June 18, 1993 - I've informed management at the halfway house that I need to go to Vancouver for a few months and take care of my friend who's sick and dying of AIDS. They will hold my position for when I get back. My flight to Vancouver is at 8:30 PM tonight.

June 20, 1993 - Ray picked me up at the airport when I arrived last night. By the time we got to his place, it was time for him to go to bed. He's been running his own company for the past few years, Can-Am Air Conditioning, so he has an early start in the morning. Ray gave me a heads up about how shocked I will be when I see Joe. I woke up early this morning, had a cup of tea and eventually got ready to walk over to Joe's place. I called first to let him know I was on my way. I had put all negative thoughts about seeing Joe out of mind; however, on arrival I approached his apartment building with much trepidation. I had not given any thought to how uncomfortable this might be for Joe or me, or how difficult it might be for him to open his door and allow me in. I thought I would just be happy to see him, and he would be just as happy to see me. I buzzed Joe's suite. It took a bit of time for him to answer. I said "Hi, it's me."

In a weak voice he said, "Come on up," and buzzed me in. Stepping out of the elevator, knocking on his door, and waiting for

Joe to answer was distressing. Mickey and Ray were right. Joe's appearance was shocking. He was a rack of bones wrapped in his burgundy, terry cloth housecoat.

Joe said, "Scary, eh?" ... I said, "No, but thin and sick looking, yes." ... We moved onto his balcony with its million dollar view. It was a nice enough day. Joe sat with his face to the wind. He said the wind helps him breathe more easily. He said he hadn't heard from two close friends in the past few months and was very hurt by it. This week he was questioning his worth as a person while on this earth. We talked about it and ended up laughing. He joked, at least he can proudly say, as a man he got to wear some really pretty dresses. In the end, we agreed that he should be proud. I teared up when he was telling me about his visit with his mom. He smoked pot in front of her. He said at first it felt odd smoking in front of her, but she understood it helped with his pain and appetite. He asked her to smoke pot with him, but she wouldn't. He told his mother what she can do for him is to not let the family refer to him as that fruit that died from that gay disease. He wants her to tell them that he is her gay son who died of AIDS and it's not a gay disease. He suggested his mother confide in those close to her so she has support when he passes. She said she had already done so. Joe doesn't want to go home now for a visit because he's looking too thin and sickly. He would rather they remember him the way he was. The only medication he's taking is one pill for the herpes sores that line the inside of his stomach and morphine for the pain. He says he knows exactly when his four hours are up and it's time to pop another morphine pill. While sitting on the balcony and smoking pot, we watched two middle-aged Asian ladies going in and coming out of the apartment building across from us. They were moving out or helping someone else move. With each trip out of the building the two carried armfuls of stuff that they shoved into their parked car. In no time, Joe and I had them pegged as the Asian Thelma and Louise and what they were packing into the car was everything they were taking with them on their weekend camping trip. We debated which one was Thelma and which one was Louise, but it became obvious when the one lady came out of the building carrying a microwave. She was obviously Thelma, the ditzy one. Who else would take a microwave on a camping trip? The other lady, Louise, came out carrying a child's tricycle. Joe and I decided that was obviously for their quick getaway.

Before leaving, Joe wanted me to walk with him the few blocks over to Main Street so he could go to the bank. He was slow moving and unsteady on his feet. He did his best to hide his frailty. While at the bank, I watched him snap at someone for staring at him. He hated being stared at. After the bank, we started walking back towards his apartment. We moved slow but steady and halfway there Joe became irritated with himself. He had wanted to stop in at the 7-Eleven to buy a Popsicle. The morphine gives him serious dry mouth and Popsicles provide relief. Joe waited on the sidewalk while I hurried back to the 7-Eleven. When I returned, I handed the Popsicle over to Joe and immediately knew it was a dumb move on my part. I should have first broken the Popsicle in two. Now that Joe had the Popsicle there was no way in hell he was giving it back to me. It was his opportunity to prove that he was stronger than he appeared and quite capable of breaking the damn Popsicle in half. I had no choice but to stand back and watch. Joe put all his strength into breaking that fucking Popsicle in two but couldn't. The Popsicle ended up breaking into several pieces and fell onto the ground except for one small piece that remained on the one stick. Joe stood so vulnerable before me and in the moment I sensed he absolutely hated me.

Watching Joe wrestle with the frozen Popsicle was a flashback moment for me. I was there before with Roger, but instead of a Popsicle it was a child's party balloon. Roger was sick and I was at his place decorating the house and blowing up balloons for his fortieth birthday. Roger sat at the kitchen table watching and decided he would help by blowing up a few balloons. I can still see Roger sitting at the end of the kitchen table trying with all his might to blow up a balloon. He didn't have the lung power. Man versus kid's party balloon and kid's party balloon won. It confirmed to Roger how sick he was. He started crying and became really angry, "Here I am a grown man and I can't even blow up a fucking kid's balloon." It was a sad and haunting memory, similar to watching Joe wrestle with the frozen Popsicle.

Joe and I slowly made our way back to his apartment in silence. I figured he had enough for one day. When I was leaving he demanded his house keys back and made it quite clear to me, "And don't you think you're moving in here Mrs. Hamilton and taking over, because you're not." I showed him where I had placed his house keys on the counter, gave him a big hug and told him I'd be back tomorrow. I sensed he hated me even more at that moment and just wanted to tell me to stay the fuck away. Unlike with Roger, I wasn't going to let Joe keep me at a distance. Not without a fight.

June 22, 1993 - I came back and Joe thankfully let me in. I convinced him to get out of the house and come to a matinee showing of Jurassic Park with Janice and myself. I had already seen it the night before leaving Toronto. When I first suggested it, Joe snapped at me. He already told me he was not going anywhere near the West End. I reminded him the theatre was downtown on Granville Street and not in the West End. He reluctantly came along and of course, we all loved the movie. Afterwards, we went back to Joe's place and had a bar-b-q on the balcony. Joe tired quickly. It was a big day for him. Janice and I left shortly after cleaning up. I went to the Royal, hung out and drank three beers. That's all it took. I went back to Ray's place and cried and cried thinking about Joe.

June 25, 1993 - Joe was sick, lying on the sofa, and looking like he wanted to die. He had no energy and no interest in living. I cleaned his place but not before asking permission. Joe said it was not necessary as he has a lady volunteer from PWA (People with AIDS) who comes in once a week and cleans for him. Joe likes her and says he looks forward to her weekly visit. There were dead leaves from his plants on the carpet that had collected over the week. I offered to pick them up but Joe said the leaves were okay on the carpet for now. Dead leaves on Joe Butler's carpet were never okay with the Joe Butler I knew. We both laughed over that. He gave in and let me clean for him. He said if I wanted to wipe his splashy shit stains off his toilet seat then go ahead and have a field day. I did. I also did laundry and laughed when putting his socks away. He heard me and asked what was so funny. I told him the difference between his sock drawer and mine was like night and day. How my socks come out of the dryer is how they go into the drawer; loose, some inside out and unmatched. Joe's socks were perfectly folded and aligned. He told me to just toss his socks into the drawer as it didn't matter anymore. No. It still mattered. They weren't perfect, but I folded his socks as best I could and placed them in the aligned rows. His Hollywood apartment looked fab-u-lous when I was done and I felt good knowing he appreciated it.

June 26, 1993 - The difference a day makes. Today Joe is off the couch and in a better mood. After lunch, I washed the dishes and he dried them. He said yesterday was a bad day and he had wished he was dead. He was annoyed with me about us being at the movie the other day. People he didn't want to see were there and he had warned me about not wanting the West End queens seeing him. I reminded him that he was well liked in the drag community and the Waitresses were a respected trio. He had no reason to fear the West End queens or be ashamed. I asked him what he thought the queens would say. If he thought their gossip would be nasty or empathetic. He didn't answer. I argued they would have nothing but empathy for him. The queens get it. They know the scene all too well. Too many in the West End have lost too many friends and lovers already to AIDS. I think Joe got it. That night, Leroy, Mickey, Joe, and I went to see the Tina Turner bio, "What's Love Got to Do with It". We all loved it. It was so encouraging seeing Joe up and around.

June 27, 1993 - One of our first nice days of summer. We smoked some pot, ate lunch at Wendy's and took Baby out for a spin with the soft top down. We drove towards the UBC Endowment Lands and down into the Southlands, always a beautiful scenic drive. While stopped at a red light and waiting for it to change, I looked over at Joe sitting in the passenger seat with his face to the wind and in that moment I didn't see HIV, or AIDS, or sickness. All I saw was my good friend Joe. He saw me looking at him and he asked, "What?" I told him I was seeing him for the first time and not his sickness, and beyond the condition his condition was in, it was still just him. He smiled. "That's right," he said. "It's just little old me. Stick boy Joe." He often called himself that. Knowing I saw him and not the disease reassured Joe. In that moment it felt like any unease between us evaporated and we were back to our usual selves. Then the stoplight turned green. We continued on our drive, with Joe keeping his head up and face to the breeze.

Back at Joe's place, we sat on the balcony and chatted. Joe said he really never knew long-term love. He knows love from his friends and family but not the love and affection from a lover. All is good though he said, as you don't miss what you never had. Joe resents his loss of independence. He admitted that's why he dried the dishes yesterday. He needs to still have some control over his life. I told him Roger bounced back from being sick and he can too. He just can't lie on the couch and wait to die. The Joe I know doesn't give up. A few days of lying on the couch and feeling pissed off at the world is okay, but not too many. He said he took a lot of sleeping pills last night hoping he'd not wake up this morning. I joked he should at least feel well rested. He said he needed it. He confessed that he hated me for coming from Toronto and showing up at his door. He didn't want me seeing him looking the way he does.

While sitting on the balcony, Joe pointed out this guy whom he claims stole parts off his car and said when he feels better the guy's going to have four flat tires. I told him to use that as an incentive to get better. When I left, Joe gave me a long, meaningful embrace. I think I left him feeling a lot safer and maybe a little less scared. Both of us had a fabulous day.

July 3, 1993 - We celebrated Canada Day with a bar-b-q at Joe's place. The balcony is wide and long enough for everyone to hang out on. There was myself, Joe, Janice, Mickey, Dale (Tuesday Night), and Joe's new friend, Kyle. When Joe had gossip to share with me, he would always first warn - "Now you know how I don't like to repeat gossip - so I'm only going to tell you once." Kyle was an Edmonton queen but now living in Vancouver. His mother recently died and left him a ton of cash which he was having a good time spending. He bought Joe and himself four hundred dollar dresses to wear at Edmonton's Coronation Ball. Kyle was also HIV positive and dying of AIDS but looked healthier than Joe. We celebrated the afternoon in our usual way; drinking, smoking pot, sharing stories, laughing, and eating hotdogs and hamburgers. Joe even modeled his new four hundred dollars dress for us. He liked it that with his new weight gain the dress hung much better on him. When talking about old movies I mentioned that Lillian Gish had recently died at the age of ninety-nine. Joe joked he might be dying but he at least outlived Lillian Gish.

"And she was ninety-nine years old."

It didn't have to make sense. We all laughed anyway. After the bar-b-q, we went to the Dairy Queen for ice cream and then Joe gave Dale and Kyle a ride home in the West End. When driving into the West End I thought, another bridge crossed.

July 15, 1993 – Joe's looking and feeling much better. Improvement is slow but sure. We're eating at Wendy's almost every second day. Thank God I'm going to the gym.

For Ray's birthday on the 13th, we had a fun bar-b-q in his back yard. The regulars were there and as usual we enjoyed each other's company. At one point, Joe did his Bette Davis bit from the film Dark Victory. In the movie, Bette Davis's character is dying from an inoperable brain tumor and as told by her doctor, moments before she dies, she'll go blind. This occurs in the final scene, while in her flower garden on a hot summer day. So, on any given hot summer day, it's not unlike Joe to stick his arm out into the direct sunlight and with the sound of much concern in his voice, announce, "Oh my. How odd? The sun seems to have gone behind the clouds, yet I can still feel its heat upon my arm." And then gasp for air like it's his last breath. It always makes me chuckle. Joe also has a Katherine Hepburn bit he likes doing because it's funny, but so wrong. He'd seen some queen do it at an Out Of Town Show and thought it was so odd that he never forgot it and often repeated it. Shaking his head and with a quiver in his voice, mimicking Katherine Hepburn - "As I used to say to my dear friend Spencer Tracy. Spencer! Shit in my mouth if you can hit it."

July 29, 1993 - Joe got a call from his doctor. He might have to go into the hospital for a blood transfusion. He thinks this is the start of the end. Mickey told me that's what it was like for his partner. It started with blood transfusions and in two months he was dead. There are so many young people dying from this horrible disease. We are gay so it doesn't matter. That's still the attitude from politicians.

Sunday, August 1, 1993 - Gay Pride! Janice, Joe, and I stood along Beach Avenue to watch the gay pride parade. It was awesome as always. Joe looks so much better with his weight gain and he's feeling alive again. I teared up as I always do when the Proud Parents of Gay Children passed by. I wondered how Joe felt being an observer rather than a participant in the parade, which he had been for so many years. After the parade, Joe went for something to eat with his Waitresses friend Robbin, who's visiting from Montreal. I went for a workout and then headed to the Royal for beers and a party. It was a hot day outside and much hotter inside the jam-packed bar. I immediately ran into Ben who was there with his new American boyfriend Tony. The two of them are living in Tony's camper van. No need to pay rent when you have a home on wheels, thus more money for cocaine and alcohol. As soon as I said hello to Ben, he handed me a hit of acid. He was passing it out like candy to anyone and everyone. He said most of the room was high. Shortly after dropping acid I was in the back of Tony's camper van, snorting two large rails of cocaine. I left before the bar was closed down by the Fire Marshal for being overcrowded. Several patrons protested with a sit-in in front of the bar and in the middle of Granville Street. Ben proudly claimed ownership for the sit-in, saying the protesters were all too high from the acid he and Tony were handing out.

August 15, 1993 - Joe's stomach is sore from the herpes lining the inside of it and he's having a hard time eating. He still has difficulty breathing and farts a lot. He said when he was at the Edmonton Ball he overheard Chatty Kathy telling others that was most likely the last time they would see him alive. That was hard for Joe to hear. He has booked a flight home to see his family. I suspect the next time he goes home it'll be as ashes in an urn.

August 26, 1993 - Joe, Mickey, and I went to The Old Spaghetti Factory in Gastown last night to celebrate our summer together. Joe looked good, definitely much better than when I first arrived. He leaves today for Saskatchewan to visit his family. I'm pleased for him. His mom will see him looking so much healthier than the last time she saw him. That should be somewhat reassuring for her.

This afternoon, Mickey and I drove Joe to the airport. He looked good and was feeling good about himself and going home. He wore his oversized jeans and a shirt over a white turtle neck sweater. He claims the layering hides his stick-boy figure. I was sad to see Joe go but I was happy for the summer we had together. When he gets back, I'll be back in Toronto.

August 28, 1993 - I ran into Ben and Tony tonight. They've been doing ecstasy for three days straight. Ben is looking thin. He said that's because of his drug use and not HIV or AIDS. The night before I left Vancouver, we had a going away bar-b-q in Ray's back yard. It was wonderful as usual with good conversation, good laughs, good food, and good people. That was the last of several great bar-b-q's we've had at Ray's place over the summer. I enjoyed taking care of his house, cats and most wonderful dog, Tosha. Joe and I had a wonderful summer together; hanging out, talking, smoking pot, eating at Wendy's, going to the movies, and taking rides in Baby with the soft top down. He was tired lots, and cranky some, but we made it through and the end result was special and meaningful.

September 2, 1993 – It was sad leaving my friends behind, but I'm back in Toronto, in time for the showing of our final short films. My short film was just okay, much like my time at the film centre, but it will look good on my resume.

I spent the afternoon writing and at some point spoke with Joe. He said he had a great time at home. His sister came to his mom's house for a visit and the husband sent his best. Joe told his mother that he'll write a letter to his sister's husband and tell him exactly what he thinks of him. Joe doesn't care if he reads it or not but he will give the brother-in-law a piece of his mind. He doesn't care if the family gets mad because he's going to be dead soon anyway. He said his health is as good as can be expected, and Baby is running fine. He said he had a wonderful summer with me, and sometimes we don't realize what we've had until it's gone. He thanked me for the time spent together and said he loved me. I know that was not easy for him to say. I told him I felt the same. I appreciated being a big part in what could be Joe's last summer.

October 17, 1993 - Spoke with Ray and Leroy. They're finally splitting up. Leroy got his own apartment and he's doing well, considering. "Considering" is an often used word for us these days. Leroy's in a lot of pain because of his feet and legs. Its HIV related. He said his feet are swollen and there are red spots on his feet that have spread up to his ankles. The poor guy is only twenty-three and staring at the end of his life. Ray is doing fine. He has a cold. Unfortunately, his buddy Michael's in the hospital and sick with HIV.

October 23, 1993 - Ray called. He still has a bad cold. He went for an HIV test and it came back negative. Thank you, God. Ray saw Joe recently and said Joe's looking pretty bad. After speaking with Ray, I phoned Joe. He had the warts burned off his face today and next weekend he's going to Portland to do drag with his friend Kyle.

November 3, 1993 - I talked to Joe later in the day. He went to the hospital to get his ass checked out and all he got was an eight or ten hour run around. A surgeon told him there is nothing that can be done for him. He might have to get a colostomy bag. He didn't like the sound of that.

November 7, 1993 - Joe has lymphoma. There is a large lump on the inside of his rectum and he'll be going for six chemotherapy treatments, twice a week. He's still in shock, but hopeful and not happy about the prospects of losing his hair. I said," This from a man who has a trunk full of long, fabulous, wigs."

He said, "And one that is near real hair."

Too funny. I can see it too, Joe sitting on the sofa wearing a long, red-haired wig and very proud of the fact that it's nearly real hair. His doctor started him on steroids. Kyle was with Joe in the doctor's office when the doctor told him the steroids will more than likely make him cranky. Joe said when the doctor told him that, he and Kyle looked at each other and said in unison, "More cranky? Is that even possible?" One thing's for certain, he's not giving up on hope or humour. It's all he has left. It must be so fucking scary for him. I can only imagine how frightening an experience all this must be.

November 10, 1993 - I phoned Joe to wish him a happy thirty-fifth birthday. He said he was sitting around feeling sorry for himself and not in a good mood. He was up all night and couldn't get to sleep with his mind racing. He said someone tried to break into his truck and on Friday he goes for his first chemo treatment. He's still in shock over the last week's news of finding out he has lymphoma. I will send him flowers on Sunday.

November 13, 1993 - Joe had his first chemo treatment on Friday and said mine was about the twelfth phone call so far today. He does not want anyone seeing him right now. He said he's tired of the whole thing and doesn't give a fuck about it anymore but was appreciative for the support he has around him. His mother called and he cried on her shoulder. He's scared, tired and fed up. His ex, Vernon, phoned but Joe refused to let him visit. He doesn't want Vernon seeing him the way he looks. He said he had a rough day today and the past week was one of the worst weeks of his life. He's angry that he's not going to have a longer life.

November 16, 1993 - Joe called last night. His voice is a bit fucked up from taking chemo. He said he's not experienced any nausea, but he has the shits and his sleep is erratic. He's decided not to attend another Coronation Ball. He's just too sick. When he went to the ball in Portland, he saw a queen who was wearing a backless dress and she looked awful. He doesn't want to look like that. He's even more self-conscious about his physical appearance. It was good talking with him. I love Joe and miss being with him very much.

November 17, 1993 - Mickey called. Joe went into the hospital today. I pray this is not a long, painful process for him.

November 18, 1993 - I called Ray this morning. Joe's okay. He was dehydrated from the endless diarrhea. They're keeping him in the hospital over the weekend and a specialist will see him on Monday. He's on morphine for pain.

November 24, 1993 - Joe called from the hospital. He sounded great. He's in good spirits, glad to be alive, and ecstatic his trip to the hospital was just about dehydration. He can handle that. His white cell count is down and he has to wait for Eeny, Meeny, Miny, and Moe to make their reappearance before receiving more chemo. He's sure the treatment is working. When he lies on his side he can tell the lump in his rectum has gone down. He'll stay in the hospital until he's well enough to go home. He's in a room with four other guys and he's the healthiest of the bunch, so he cranks their beds up and down for them and helps them anyway he can. He appreciates his many visitors but some stay way too late. I told Joe if he needs me at any time I will come out. I was happy after talking with him. The devil is winning the battle but the war's not over yet.

I spoke with Ray. Leroy's in the hospital because of complications with his legs and feet. Ray said Joe lies in his hospital bed with the TV guide in one hand and the small TV up close to his face. In one visit, Ray saw Joe, Leroy, and Michael. He said he doesn't have to go far to meet friends anymore. It's like the hospital has replaced the gay bar.

December 1, 1993 - Joe called to let me know he's home from the hospital. It was not that bad an experience even though the chemo treatments have caused his hair to fall out in chunks. He sounded great and enthusiastic. Of course, we joked about his chemo treatments and laughed. If we don't laugh, we cry. He said he can't die yet as he has too much TV watching to get in. He's lost more weight and is down to one hundred and four pounds. His herpes sores start at the roof of his mouth, line his esophagus, and go down into his stomach. He hates taking pills. He said every time he takes a pill it's a reminder of the condition his condition is in.

December 6, 1993 - I saw the movie Philadelphia. It fucking devastated me. I bawled my eyes out and left before the house lights came up. I came home and called Joe. I told him I saw the movie and how upset it made me and that I just wanted to call and say hi. He thought I was being overly sentimental.

December 15, 1993 - Joe called. He was stressed out and anxious about going home to his parents' place for Christmas. This will be his last Christmas and going home will be to say goodbye. He's self-conscious about his appearance and that adds to his apprehension over facing the family. He says he's a shell of a man. He has no body hair and shaves once a week. His herpes sores are mostly gone from his mouth, but his stomach still aches from them. When he gets back after Christmas, he'll go into the hospital for a round of intravenous drugs and that should hopefully heal his stomach. We talked about death. He's scared but sees it as a welcome relief. He said he was glad to hear from me. He has a lot of anger and rightfully so. His doctor told him he has at most six months to live. It's important to Joe that he makes it through this Christmas so in future Christmases his death won't be a painful reminder for his family.

December 17, 1993 - Joe said each time he looks in the mirror it's another painful reminder. He's in a lot of pain, exhausted, and tired of fighting. The stigma of AIDS is a large cause of his emotional pain. He said if it wasn't for the stigma of having AIDS, dying would be a whole lot easier.

When speaking with Ray, he said Joe farts all the time. It doesn't matter where he is, or who's around him, he farts and he stinks like hell.

December 21, 1993 - I called Joe when I got home from work last night. He sounded a lot better. He was stressed out to the max about going home for Christmas so he decided against it. He's immensely relieved. He'll check himself into the hospital in the next day or two. I think of Roger's last trip home to see his family and how he backed out at the last minute. I wonder if his family knows he's passed away.

December 25, 1993 - Christmas Day - Joe's out of the hospital on a day pass and he's going to Miss Tuesday Night's place for dinner. He has four loonie-sized ulcers at the top and bottom of his esophagus. They took tests and he'll find out the results later. He goes back into the hospital tomorrow.

January 16, 1994 - Spoke with Joe. He was in good spirits. They stopped the chemo treatments as he's not reacting well to them. The lump in his rectum is still there but isn't getting any larger. He's urinating blood which is the result of the chemo on his bladder. The pain is manageable thanks to plenty of morphine. He's been home since Thursday but expects to be back in the hospital in no time. He said he has a stack of Seconal and might end it all if life gets too unbearable. He's not there yet. I wish I could be there with him but financially I can't afford it right now. He understands.

February 1, 1994 - Spoke with Ray and Joe. Ray's doing well. Joe was in a good mood. The only pills he's on right now are steroids for lymphoma, morphine for pain, and one pill for something else. He said he's tired of being weak and sick, but mentally he's doing better.

February 13, 1994 - Ray called and told me Michael died last night. That's so sad. Poor Ray. He and Michael were really close buddies. Ray will miss him dearly.

February 22, 1994 - They spread Michael's ashes. His family is taking it very hard. Michael was only twenty-seven years old and now dead from AIDS. It seems if you're gay and make it past forty, you should consider yourself lucky.

February 23, 1994 - Spoke with Joe tonight before going to work at the halfway house. He's depressed, sick and has a sore stomach. The last couple of days have not been fun. I tried to lift his spirits. We managed a few laughs. Joe said he lies there waiting to die. He will sell his truck as he can't afford two vehicles and he's using neither. He's upset about putting Baby away. He said he can't lift the hood any longer. It's too heavy for him. But he did take her for one last drive the other day. Joe told me Ray's feeling down over Michael's death.

February 28, 1994 - Ray called Sunday night. He was feeling an acute sense of loss and grief over Michael's death. We chatted. All we can do is learn to live with our grief and be there for each other. I wish I was there to give Ray a big hug. Michael's gone except for the memories.

March 29, 1994 - Spoke with Ray and Leroy. Ray is off to Palm Springs. Leroy said his feet are really bad and they might have to amputate. The poor kid's taking liquid morphine for the severe pain. He's happy though he says. According to Leroy, Joe is a really changed person these days. He's no longer bitter and angry but calmer and more relaxed.

April 15, 1994 - I picked up Xtra, Toronto's gay newspaper, and in the "Proud Lives" section was Matthew Cohan's name and photo. Matthew was a former college classmate who we suspected of being gay. I was shocked and sad to see Matthew's face there.

I felt awful last night and today, depressed and a bit lost. I called Ray and Joe and spoke with them and that made me feel better. Joe said his sister called and she can't bear to see him the way he is now. It would be too painful. He understands.

April 27, 1994 - The last time I talked to Joe, he was not feeling well. We managed our few laughs. He said his buddy Kyle has Kaposi's sarcoma internally and that's really not good. Kyle is also infected with the blindness disease. There's very little they can do for him. I pray he does not suffer too much. Joe has spots on his face and they're treated by injecting chemo into the sores. Joe and I chatted about my depression last week. I was so fucking depressed.

I could see no light and felt lost. Fortunately, I know there are always better days ahead.

May 5, 1994 - Joe remains scared and not feeling well, but he's hanging on. It was great to hear from him. He's giving Baby to his brother. His brother will pick Baby up and drive her back home to Saskatchewan. He gave the truck to Ray. This has made Joe very sad. He said it's been hard on him giving away his vehicles. These are more signs of his end closing in. He says Kyle is sick but holding up.

May 14, 1994 - Last week I was on a self-destructive path. I couldn't stop myself. I was out every night, smoking pot, drinking beer and looking to get laid. I went to the baths three times. I reminded myself it's not where you play but how you play. At least, no matter how low I feel, I always play safe. The baths scare me, but I can't tell myself no.

I was talking to Ray and Joe. Ray has met this twenty-nine-year-old. I hope this one works out for him.

May 17, 1994 - Ray called to tell me he visited Joe at the hospital last night. Joe's doctor told Joe it's time to decide if he wants to die at home or in the hospital. I told Ray if Joe wants to die at home, I'll come to Vancouver and take care of him. Ray said that's a big responsibility. I'm good with it. Joe deserves to die at home in his fab-u-lous Hollywood apartment. I have no idea what to expect, but I'll cross that bridge when I get there.

I wiped tears from my eyes all day. What broke my heart was Ray telling me that Joe doesn't want this to happen. He's not ready. He's frightened. He doesn't want to die. Ray will see Joe this afternoon. I told him to call me as soon as his visit's over.

Ray called after his visit with Joe. Joe's decided that he wants to go home to die so he can smoke all the pot he wants and watch TV on a bigger screen. Spoke with Mickey. We talked a lot about Joe and what he's about to go through. Having recently gone through this with his partner of eighteen years, it has to be challenging for Mickey to go through this once again. Mickey said Joe cried a lot today. He told Joe he has to die at home because there's better parking at his place than at the hospital. That's funny. Joe's relieved I'm coming to take care of him but concerned about my job. I can always get another job.

May 19, 1994 - I informed the assistant director at the halfway house that I needed to take a month or so off so I can go back to Vancouver and take care of my best friend dying of AIDS. She said it must be awful to have a friend dying of AIDS and he's not even gay. Like being gay is deserving and being straight is not. I was surprised she would even say such a cunty thing. I politely corrected her. Her face turned red from embarrassment.

May 24, 1994 - Ray called. Joe's coming home from the hospital today. His brother and his wife will pick him up at the hospital and stay with him until the end of the week. I'm taking a 9 pm flight to Vancouver.

May 25, 1994 - I called Joe around 9 AM and we agreed I'd visit him in the early afternoon. When I got there, the building manager was in the lobby and she asked about Joe. She hadn't realized how sick he was and was sincerely concerned. I walked into Joe's apartment, gave him a hug and then we sat and chatted about not much. It was awkward with his brother and wife there. I knew of them but didn't know them. Joe was in a good mood despite his illness. He's fragile and extremely thin. His hair was short and dark. I thought because of the chemo he would be bald. He actually looked better than I expected. He said he was relieved to be out of the hospital. There was a prescription for him at the pharmacy, so his brother and wife offered to pick it up and give us time together. They said they'd be back in a few hours. As we talked, Joe lay on the pull out couch in the living room. He's accepted death is inevitable so he might as well just go with it. We talked about my staying with him and that this is about him and his comfort. I asked him to let me know what he wants, needs, and does not approve of. I gave him a card about planting a seed of friendship and it growing larger than the two of us. We talked about our time together as friends and hardly being apart since 1981. He was sorry I had left my job again on his account. When I helped him go to the washroom, I got to see how incredibly frail he really was. He was embarrassed when I had to wipe his ass. The trip to the bathroom exhausted him. He said his spine, chest, and lungs were sore. He made a comment about how skinny his legs were. I don't think my poor friend Joe will survive much longer. Joe laid back on the sofa bed and coughed now and then. He really tries to put up a good front. His building manager dropped off flowers.

May 27, 1994 - Early afternoon and I'm sitting at Joe's place. The TV is on. Joe's brother and his wife are getting ready to drive back home. Thank God they're going so I can properly care for Joe. His family has definitely been there for him but they don't understand the level of care Joe needs. His brother said they'll leave around 3 pm unless Joe wants them to stay. Joe said no. Joe feels he needs to stay awake and interact with them even though he doesn't have that energy to spare. While Joe and his brother were having a private moment in the living room, I had a chat with the wife in the kitchen. She said I must have lost a lot of friends. She said as hard as it is for Joe's brother to leave, he knows it's time for Joe and his friends to be together. Before saying their final goodbyes, his brother and wife took a walk to the store. He's having a hard time leaving. Joe asked me what more can he do for his brother. I suggested he tell his brother that he loves him and to give him his high school ring before he leaves. He had commented on the ring earlier. Joe said he'll give him the ring. It's very sad.

Joe's brother and wife returned. We watched a movie and afterwards, his brother was more at ease with leaving. It was painful for Joe to watch them drive away in Baby.

Joe can't eat much. I served mashed potatoes, creamed corn, and apple sauce for supper. He ate some, took his pills and now he's out of it. I see the effect of the morphine on him. He tries to remember what day it is, what show is on TV and asks if it's the TV he's watching or a video.

May 28, 1994 – I'm staying with Joe at his place and sleeping in his bed. Joe prefers the chesterfield in the living room so he can watch TV. I woke up several times during the night to the hissing sound of the TV being off the air. Joe called out for me around 1:30 AM. He needed water. He's frail today. He's not yet used to me doing things for him. We talked about his loss of independence and how much he resents it. I was insecure for a moment this morning about our friendship. I was feeling like I was doing this without any appreciation from Joe and thinking how he appreciates his other friends more than me. How stupid of me. Fortunately, the feeling passed quickly. I washed him, brushed his teeth, put lotion on his body and dressed him in a nice colourful t-shirt. I tidied and cleaned his place, put fresh flowers in a vase and set up the lovely cards his friends and family had sent. There is a nice photo of his sister with her kids at his bedside. His sister called. She's very sad. She's sending flowers on Monday. Joe still can't eat anything. I think he's in a lot of pain and not saying anything. Swallowing his meds is difficult. Everything goes right through him. Considering he eats nothing, he certainly shits a lot. I did laundry and we watched A Perfect World, with Clint Eastwood. At one point, Joe asked if I'm freaked out yet. I said no. I told him my heart goes out to him and all his friends feel the same. I told him we loved him. I also told him when friends come to visit he doesn't need to play host. I will do that. He can sleep as much as he needs. We talked about Svend Robinson and how gay positive he is as a personality and public figure. He's our Harvey Milk. Shortly after eight this evening, Janice popped over for a visit and the three of us smoked pot. I don't know if the pot was the cause, but soon afterwards Joe got scared. He asked me to sit beside him on the bed and hold his hand. He started to cry. The intercom buzzed and it was Leroy popping over for a visit. Janice was freaked out by Joe's crying, decided to leave and said she would catch up with Leroy in the foyer and tell him it wasn't a good time to visit. I lay beside Joe on the bed, held his hand and comforted him. He repeated my name over and over, "Oh, Bobby. Bobby. Bobby." He cried out for his mother and to God. His cry was loud. I wondered what the neighbours were thinking. Joe sobbed for me to help him but there was nothing I could do. I asked him if he preferred to go to the hospital but he said no. We lay together for some time and I continued to hold his hand and comfort him the best I could. I told Joe to let go, not to hold on, not to be scared. I prayed for God to take Joe and spare him any more pain and fear. I held him into the early hours of the morning. He slept off and on. I got very little sleep. Joe woke up at one point and asked, "Am I dead yet?" I said I hoped not because that would mean I was dead too. We chuckled. He said he looks like an AIDS victim. I couldn't disagree. I'll sleep with him on the couch from now on. I don't want to leave him alone.

May 29, 1994 - Joe has no interest in eating and remains lying on the pull out couch. He said he feels the end is really close and apologized for his freaking out last night. He questioned why he did it. I told him he definitely had nothing to apologize for or be sorry about. If it was me in his position, I would still be in a state of hysteria and it wouldn't look pretty. Joe talked about his mother. He's concerned for her and how painful his death will be for her. He wants me to call his mom and tell her to get here soon. Joe told me who to call when he passes on. He's instructed me on who gets what. He said not to let his parents take everything because they will. He's so weak and frail but fully aware and alert.

Joe's brother called. They made it home safely. Joe ate one Popsicle all day. Regardless, he continues to pass a lot of shit. The herpes is hard on his rectum and cleaning his bottom is painful for him. The first diaper was a totally embarrassing moment for Joe, but we've gotten over that. Tonight he said he was scared. We talked about Gramma and Joe being with him when he died. This is all so, so, so sad. At the moment, Joe's lying on the sofa bed, wearing his eye glasses and dressed in an orange t-shirt, pale yellow pajama bottoms and white socks. One leg is up, bent at the knee and shaking. He was to have company but was not up to it. People call and ask how Joe's doing, but that's an awkward conversation to have with him in the room.

May 30, 1994 - I called Joe's mother. She and Joe's stepfather will arrive later this evening. We had an okay night. We were up until about 2 AM and then up again around five or six. Neither of us had much sleep. Joe had a few small seizures during the night. I stayed by his side and talked calmly to him until they ended. I didn't know what else to do. At times he was scared and cried out, questioning, "Why?" He gave me a scare with a seizure he had earlier this morning. At one point, I thought he was a goner. Since then he's been very talkative. Joe's buddy Kyle dropped in. For a short period, Joe was able to chat and make sense, but then he suddenly switched and became very chatty and animated. Who's on TV? Who is in the room? Nothing connected. He had a childlike innocence. He's been calling for his mom. Joe seems aware of what's being said but unable to control his thought patterns. I think he's going blind as well. I was standing in front of him this morning and he asked me where I was. The diarrhea seems to have stopped. Right now he's lying on the sofa bed randomly talking and in a playful mood.

As the afternoon progressed, Joe got tired and quietly regressed. He can't last much longer. Kyle picked up Joe's mom and stepfather at the airport around 8:30 PM. Unfortunately for his mother, Joe is no longer able to carry a conversation. She was grateful he was still alive. I'd never met Joe's parents before. I'm sleeping on the sofa bed with Joe and they have the bedroom. After the parents went to bed, I went to the bathroom and when I came back, Joe was in the middle of another seizure. This one was stronger and more frightening than the others. When he came out of it, he was once again very animated and talkative and this time he started crawling around on the bed. I needed help so I called Mickey. For the next few hours, Mickey and I sat on the bed with Joe. Joe was so care free and childlike. He would repeat, "Bob, Bob, Bob."

Before Mickey got there I said to Joe, "That horrible Mrs. Saunders is on her way over to see you."

Joe pointed his finger at me and grinned, "We have to do something about her." He had a smile from ear to ear. He was very funny. It was so like Joe to continue on with, "And her little dog too!" He called for Janice and his mom. He refused to sleep. It was as if he was scared to close his eyes in case he didn't wake up. An hour or so later, Joe quieted down. By morning, I knew this would be his last day.

May 31, 1994 - In the afternoon, Joe's longtime friends with roots going back to Edmonton and the drag community showed up to pay a visit. Joe was no longer mentally there and his body continued to diminish. He laid on the sofa bed, quiet and still, seemingly in a deep sleep. I wondered if Joe's mom and stepfather were uncomfortable being in the company of all us gay boys. Their lives on a rural Saskatchewan farm are far removed from anything remotely gay. While Joe was approaching his final hours, the majority of the city, as well as those in Joe's living room, were captivated by the Stanley Cup playoffs between the Vancouver Canucks and the New York Rangers. Janice was horrified that the hockey game was on TV while Joe lay dying. She knew how much Joe hated hockey. I had no interest in the game either, but it gave

Joe's mother and stepfather a way to connect with the gay boys. I think Joe would have appreciated this more than having his parents sit around in uncomfortable silence.

In between periods, at approximately 7:15 PM, in the presence of his gay and straight family, my dear pal and best friend Joe succumbed to AIDS. Joe's doctor came to the apartment and pronounced Joe officially dead. The paramedics were quick to arrive. I watched them move Joe's body from the sofa bed to the stretcher. Witnessing how tightly they strapped down Joe's body, it was a blessing he was dead. I followed the paramedics to the elevator and watched as they quickly manoeuvered the stretcher into an upright position inside the elevator. That explained why they strapped the body down so tightly. The elevator door then closed and that was it. Joe was now forever gone. As sad as his passing was, Joe's death was a long time coming and there was comfort knowing he was in a better place. Joe died a proud gay man. I was better for knowing Joe Butler. He was my gay mentor. From our early start of hanging out together, he introduced me to all that was gay. He wasn't afraid of it like I was. He relished in it. From the start he opened my eyes and my mind wider, allowing for a better understanding of myself, gender politics and the gay community I belonged to. My only wish was that Joe could have been happier in the later part of his brief life, but then he had a lot to be angry about; from being raised by a hateful, homophobic stepfather, to contracting HIV and dying of AIDS at a time when he had so much hope and promise for a full and rewarding life. It saddens me that Joe never got the opportunity to grow into himself. Rest in peace me dear friend.

June 1, 1994 - Janice and I went to Granville Island and purchased a beautifully, Native carved wooden box to put Joe's ashes in. Shortly after arriving back at Ray's place, a small but heavy cardboard box containing Joe's ashes was delivered. I was not prepared for the texture, the weight, and the amount of what was left of my dear friend Joe after cremation. The mound of grey ashes had bone fragments throughout and I could have lived without the experience of separating Joe's ashes into two halves. Janice stood in Ray's kitchen, horrified, as she watched me use an ice cream scoop to divide Joe's ashes. Half will go home with Joe's mother for a traditional service. Joe's mother and stepfather, along with Joe's close friends, left in Ray's and his friend's boat and we motored across False Creek and out into English Bay. It was a breezy day with the sun shining. I hoped the beauty of the surroundings helped Joe's mother understand why Joe chose to have his ashes spread here. Mickey read aloud a wonderful poem. The wooden box with Joe's ashes was passed amongst us. We said our final goodbyes as we let Joe's ashes slip through our fingers and fall into the cold blue water below. What we had not anticipated was the breeze carrying some of Joe's ashes back towards us and onto the boat. I felt for Joe's mom having to watch Ray scurry about with a rag cleaning up the ashes falling onto the boat's polished white surface. After the scattering of Joe's ashes, we docked back at Stamps Landing and went for lunch. Needing to get back to the farm, Joe's mother and stepfather left the next day and drove back to Saskatchewan with most of Joe's possessions in a large rental truck.

Days Later - I submitted Joe's obituary to the "Proud Lives" section in Xtra West. I'm sure Joe had pictured his face there many times before. A friend asked if it was important that I state Joe died from AIDS. Without a doubt, there was nothing to be ashamed of. Joe would have wanted it.

June 14, 1994 - Joe put aside one thousand dollars for his celebration of life party. I organized his apartment from what was left after his parent's haul. There was plenty of pot to smoke, booze to drink, and catered food to eat. I also put a photo album together of Joe throughout the years including photos of Baby and many of him in drag. I had invited Joe's landlady to the party. After looking through the photo album, she said she would have loved to seen Joe in drag. At one point we gathered on the balcony and let go helium balloons, symbolizing Joe's spirit being set free and rising towards the heavens. While the party was in progress so was the final Stanley Cup game between the Vancouver Canucks and the New York Rangers. Janice was once again horrified knowing how much Joe hated hockey. But it was inescapable. The whole city had Stanley Cup fever. We ate, drank and partied while keeping an ear to the hockey game. The game ended with the Canucks losing and shortly afterwards a major riot broke out on Robson Street.

June 17, 1994 - Joe's friend Kyle died. He had been sick for the past two weeks and finally lost his battle to AIDS. God bless him.

I packed up, cleaned up and emptied out Joe's apartment. When I left it felt like I was closing the door on the past.

July 1, 1994 - I volunteered to help Leroy move into a one-bedroom apartment on Burnaby Street in the West End. His new place is closer to St. Paul's hospital which was a good move considering his health. His feet and legs are badly swollen and very painful as a result of vasculitis. Also, his leg muscles are deteriorating and he has a hard time standing or walking without walking canes. His doctor finally told him it's HIV-related and there is no treatment. They may have to amputate his legs. He's only twenty-five. When I arrived at the apartment Leroy was moving out of, nothing was packed or ready to go. He had been partying all night on morphine and cocaine and whatever else he got his hands on. He was lying on his futon, too sick to get it together and in no shape to help. Fortunately, I arrived before the movers and packed as fast as I could. Much later in the move, Leroy's aunt showed up to help. It was deeply upsetting to see Leroy helpless and so vulnerable. After the move, I went back to Ray's place, sat down at his desk and feeling overwhelmed I cried my fucking heart out. I was frustrated, angry, and depressed by the cruelty and unfairness of our world.

July 15, 1994 - I returned to Toronto. The night before leaving Vancouver, fourteen of us went to the Rooster's Quarters (Montreal Chicken) on Denman Street for dinner. My gay family was sincerely sad to see me leave and I was equally sad to leave my friends, but I had a job to get back to, bills to pay, and scripts to write. We all toasted Joe. He was gone but definitely not forgotten.

July 23, 1994 - I had a dream about Joe the other night. I cried afterwards. At first we were watching TV, then we were on a sidewalk in the West End, then seated inside a restaurant. The people we were sitting with were uncomfortable because Joe had told them he had AIDS. I told him we couldn't sit there. He was making people uncomfortable. Then we are at a family restaurant. It was full of families. We were sitting at a table and had finished eating. Two lesbians sitting on the bench next to Joe were carrying on with him and joking. I said we should go. The lesbians said no. At five o'clock all the families have to be finished eating and then the place turns into a gay bar/tea dance. So Joe and I stayed. Joe talked about how he loved to dance. The dream ended with Joe saying he should have cooked the chicken. I didn't have a clue what cooking the chicken meant, but I did enjoy spending time with Joe in my dream.

I was speaking with Ray and he said he has no one to talk to anymore. Ya, I hear you buddy. But we still have each other.

August 26, 1995 - Mike Harris, Premier of Ontario, introduced the "Common Sense Revolution", another word for cutting costs and as a result the halfway house where I have been working full time is scheduled to close. Instead of looking for another job in Toronto or moving back to Vancouver, I've decided to head home to northern New Brunswick, get reacquainted with my family and write for the next year while living on unemployment insurance.

November 21, 1995 - I boarded the VIA Rail train at Union Station in downtown Toronto and sat back for the eighteen hour ride home. During the trip it dawned on me that I left home when I was just shy of eighteen years old and now eighteen years later, at the age of thirty-six, I was returning. Was this me coming full circle? Was I going home to die? So many had died, so why should I be spared? Would I go home and find out I had AIDS? I was plagued with these thoughts throughout the trip.

At home, I rented a two bedroom apartment for a fraction of what it would cost in Toronto, or Vancouver. One night, I looked in the mirror and swore I could see the start of what looked like a blue spot near my upper lip. Was this Kaposi's sarcoma? Was this the start of the end? It was nothing more than my mind playing tricks on me.

Summer, 1996 - After hibernating through winter, smoking lots of hash, becoming familiar with CBC radio, reading, writing, journaling my down-home experiences and choking the chicken, I was ready by summer to check out the local gay scene. I searched out the number for the New Brunswick Gay Alliance in the phone book and called. Monthly dances were popular and I attended two dances. Both were in Bathurst, a small city within an hour's drive from my home town, Dalhousie. The first was held at a sports hall rented for the evening. There was a good turnout of gay men and lesbians. I recognized a few of the women from the girls' softball team I used to keep score for when I was in high school. A guy from my home town took an interest in me and introduced himself. He was friendly but not my type. The second dance I went to was at a bar, again rented for the evening. The guy from my home town was there. He was drunk and possibly high and asked me to dance. I politely declined. He went to the dance floor alone and I watched him dancing on his own. He danced like no one was watching and he was enraptured by the words to the Celine Dion song, "Because You Loved Me". It seemed every word spoke to his being.

"You were my strength when I was weak. You were my voice when I couldn't speak. You were my eyes when I couldn't see. You saw the best that was in me. Lifted me up when I couldn't reach. You gave me faith 'cause you believed. I am everything I am because you loved me."

Watching him being caught up in the emotion of the song touched my heart and as well saddened me. A few days later, when visiting an aunt and uncle in Moncton, I overheard my uncle asking my mother if they had found the missing guy from Dalhousie yet. Hearing his name rang a bell. My mother said he'd gone to a dance in Bathurst on Saturday night and hadn't been seen or heard from since. It was him, the same guy I had watched dancing. Days later, his body was found washed up on the beach. Apparently, he was HIV positive, sick, and depressed. It's believed after leaving the dance he went to the ocean and drowned himself. It was sad and depressing news to hear. Even in small town New Brunswick I couldn't escape the horror of AIDS.

November 1, 1996 - I turned thirty-seven and my theory about coming full circle and dying from AIDS was now debunked. I would survive. I got tested for HIV, but unlike in Vancouver and Toronto, getting tested here seemed like more of a big deal and conducted with an atmosphere of secrecy. After all my worry, I remained negative.

April, 1997 - I returned to Vancouver. Mickey had two spare bedrooms and I rented one of the rooms until I resettled. Ray bought a house on the east side and his new boyfriend moved in with him. Leroy was not doing well. HIV was taking its toll and his addiction to alcohol, cocaine, and morphine wasn't helping.

November, 1997 - I began dating someone. A month later, he informed me that he was HIV positive and said if I wanted to terminate the relationship he would understand. That was an uncomfortable conversation for him to have. I had suspected he was HIV positive and we practiced safe sex so I never felt at risk. We dated for eight months and then went our separate ways. All this time I continued to write non-stop. My screenplay, The Changing of the Guard, was optioned by a local director. Again, it would go nowhere. I didn't want to get back into the jail business and lucked out when Ray's friend set me up working as a bellman in the Dakota Hotel; a boutique style hotel in the heart of Granville's entertainment district. In the hotel's Cuban themed cigar lounge, BaBalu, the lead singer in the house band that played every weekend was a young Michael Buble.

Two years later, September, 1999 - I began working across the street as a desk clerk at The Royal Hotel. The Royal was a gay hotel and catered to working class gays and lesbians. This was my first "gay job". A friend suggested I could have applied for a similar job in a better hotel, on a better street, with better people, making better money, but the Royal had male strippers on Saturday nights, drag queens on Monday and Thursday nights, gay bingo on Tuesday nights, and all men's on Friday nights. Between the bar and the hotel, the place was 365-24-7 gay. Yes, the pay was lousy and the tips non-existent, but as a writer I couldn't wait to start journaling my experience.

One of the perks of working the front desk at the Royal was the free chat line membership cards for Bad Boys; a service where gay men hooked up over the phone. Every now and then a chubby Asian guy would pass through the hotel lobby and drop off a few cards. I had seen the ads at the back of the community newspapers but I was always too cheap to pay for the service. Now that I had free access cards, I was on the phone listening in. It quickly became addictive. It was an amusing way to spend the long and quiet winter nights at the front desk. It was also an eye-opening education. The sexual requests ran the gambit; some astonished me, others excited me and some turned me off. I hooked up a few times. One guy I hooked up with and became infatuated with would define the word "player". Our "affairette", as Joe would have called it, ended in heartache for me and ruined my friendship with Ray for a few years. One Saturday afternoon, I walked in on the player and Ray being up close and personal with each other, which I had recently started to suspect. They were sly and not upfront about it. That didn't sit well with me. In one way it was a blessing because it made it easier for me to get the monkey, that being the player, off my back. He had to go. As for Ray, the king of denial, he claimed I didn't see what I saw. All that was needed was an apology and we could have moved on, but Ray couldn't do that. So I walked away.

November, 1999 - While listening in on the chat lines, I heard an unfamiliar term: barebacking. My ever knowledgeable buddy Ben explained that barebacking was simply fucking without condoms and joked that it was the hottest new thing and I was the only one out of the loop. I was shocked to hear people were willingly practicing unsafe sex. I could understand positive men barebacking with each other. I wondered if barebacking was becoming common place and fetishized within our community, how would this affect gay men who were HIV negative? Yes, we now had the cocktail but there were still consequences with becoming HIV positive and taking such potent medication. Over the following weeks I had conversations with friends and colleagues about barebacking and we all agreed, it was becoming a "thing" and one was crazy to do it without protection, especially if you were HIV negative. Looking around the community, it appeared that the safe sex message was no longer as prevalent. After all we had been through in our very recent history with the AIDS crisis, I thought now was not the time to stop preaching safe sex. Over the weeks, I obsessed over this and finally wrote a letter to the editor of Xtra West, hoping to create a community dialogue on the subject of barebacking and at the same time serve as a reminder of the importance of safe sex. In the letter, I assumed the character of someone who barebacked and gave reasons ranging from ignorance to personal choices. I dropped my letter off at the Xtra West office and a few days later, received a phone call from the editor. I didn't answer the phone so the editor left a message. He wanted to print my letter in their next issue but first required my verbal consent. I suspected such a letter would result in a strong reaction, so I took a few days to think about whether or not I was prepared to go public and face the heat. I chickened out. The editor called a second time and left the same message. He really wanted to print my letter. I thought if I felt strongly enough to write the letter in the first place, why not take it on? I called him back, confirmed I was the author and gave him permission to print the letter. The letter titled "BAREBACKING PLEASURES", editor's headline not mine, in essence said: whatever my sexual practices, they are adult choices made between myself and my sexual partner so why should it be anyone else's concern? More and more gay men bareback and find it both liberating and gratifying. It's a return to the years before AIDS and a time of sexual freedom. People are no longer dying. The photos of loved ones no longer fill our community newspaper. I signed my name to the letter and it was published in the following issue. As suspected, my letter created a serious buzz within the community. Ben said I made myself into a social pariah. I was shunned by some. Others asked why I would even dare sign my name and why I even wrote such a letter. After explaining my reason, many were in agreement and encouraged me. And many thought I was just an asshole. Two weeks after my letter was published, three responses were printed. They ranted and preached at me for barebacking. I was called irresponsible, naive, and stupid. Two weeks later, I wrote a follow up letter explaining my actions; to bring awareness and open discussion to the risks of barebacking. The intent was to draw attention to the responsibility we have in keeping the safe sex message alive and keep it in the forefront. SILENCE EQUALS DEATH. We owed it to the new generation of young men coming out into our bars and community. I ended the letter saying hopefully my letter, the responses to it, and the ensuing conversations served such a purpose. Again, some applauded me and some still thought I was an asshole.

Spring, 2000 - Prior to working at the Royal and moving into the West End, I used to wait for my bus in front of a construction site on Granville Street. Over time, I became a familiar face to the security guard working there. He was a man of my height and stature, with salt and pepper hair, gentle demeanor, and I thought attractive. We always exchanged a few polite words, nothing too serious. He seemed shy and reserved but always said hello with a smile. When I last saw him, he was walking with the aid of a cane.

One night, around 8 PM, the security guard entered the hotel lobby. He was no longer walking with a cane but looked disheveled. His head was shaved, his finger nails long and dirty, and he carried his belongings in two green garbage bags. He wanted to rent a room for a few nights. He told me that he had fallen on hard times and living out of his van, but it was towed away. To save money, he had been living in Stanley Park for the last several months. My spider sense tingled. I didn't get a good feeling about the situation, so I tried to encourage him to go elsewhere. I quoted the maximum price for our rooms but he had enough money to pay for the room. He asked for a room with a bathtub. I told him we only had stand up showers. Nothing I said discouraged him. He was determined to stay. He said he had enough money saved to pay for his planned weekend. When he saw my reluctance to rent him a room, he made me a solemn promise he wouldn't be a problem. I remembered him for being a nice guy and in the end I made a liar of myself and gave him our best rate on a room with a bathtub for two nights. As it turned out, my spider sense was right. About an hour after checking in, he called the front desk telling me he was about to make a life changing decision and wanted to speak with me in his room. I didn't feel good about the phone call and told him I could give him five minutes. Suspecting that I might find him in drag and hanging from a light fixture, I took a box cutter with me and asked one of the bartenders to keep an eye from a distance. I knocked on his door and he told me to come in but the door was locked. He unlocked the door but didn't open it. I opened the door but didn't see him and when he spoke, it was from behind the door. I told him I wouldn't enter the room until he came out; wisdom learned from my days as a jail guard. He came out from behind the door dressed in complete drag and in a distraught state. I remained in the doorway and watched him frantically pace about the room, smoking a hand-rolled cigarette and nervously rattling off his story. The energy in the room was a tense battle going on between life and death, with sanity hanging from a fragile thread. It could snap at any moment. He told me that he never knew himself as a man but always as a woman and forever hated that thing between his legs. Living in Stanley Park was to save money for the hormones he needed to start his transition from male to female. He said he never had friends because when he hung around with someone for too long, they would always end up being freaked out by his girly behaviour. He grew tired of hiding his true nature and was now ready and willing to face the consequences, but before he would be considered for surgery, he had to out himself and live as a woman for one year. As it turned out, his mission on this night was to out himself as transgender to someone, and that someone he opted for was me. He said from our conversations in front of the construction site he felt safe with me and could trust me. At one point, he yelled at me, "This is not about sex!"

I told him I knew that. "It's about identity." He went silent. I don't think he expected me to say that and in that moment I sensed all the energy that was death, evaporated from the room. Life had won out. In her desperate moment of need, someone understood. She asked me if I found her attractive. I told her I like boys and not girls. Did I like her feminine attire? I didn't have the heart to tell her she looked like a trucker in old woman drag, so instead I told her I was sure once she got comfortable with her transition she would adopt a more fitting look. All I could do was give her a hug, wish her the best, and reassure her that she'll be okay.

The next day when I came back to work, she was sitting in the hotel lobby, still looking like a trucker in older woman drag; flower print long dress, shawl, sensible shoes and white gloves. She sat in the lobby trying to build up the courage to take her first walk in public as a woman. That walk was tantamount to her transgender freedom, but she was paralyzed by fear. As luck would have it, a hotel guest, a European leather guy, entered the lobby and saw her in distress. After hearing her situation, he offered to escort her on her walk down Granville Street. They left with her on his arm and returned about half an hour later. They had walked a few blocks down Granville Street to Starbucks, got a coffee to go and returned to the hotel lobby where she sat back down. She was proud of herself for making it that far. I watched her firmly grasping her cup of coffee in her trembling hands. She smiled and proudly exclaimed, "At least I didn't spill any coffee on my white gloves."

2004 - Vancouver's AIDS memorial was erected at Sunset Beach, overlooking English Bay. Among the many names on the solid metal panels is, Joe Butler. He would approve.

Several years later - While walking to work one day, Joe popped into my head and I thought of how old he was when he died. Now in my fifties, I realized for the first time just how young thirty-five was. It saddened me to think Joe was in the prime of his life. But we were all so young then.

HEROES

Those

who lost

their lives

in battle

the war

called AIDS

EPILOGUE

Summer, 2020 - Here we are in the midst of another global pandemic, Covid-19. In early March, I noted in my diary that because of PrEP, not a cure, but a one pill a day solution to preventing HIV, we were back to fucking like it was the 70's again. I wondered how long this period of sexual freedom would last. Two weeks later we were on lockdown.

The Wall

Joe and Jean

Me, summer 1977

Paul and Robbin

Joe and Ray

Roger

Baby

Joe in drag, 1981

Me, Edmonton Remand Centre, 1979

Michael

Me and Ray 1982   Ted

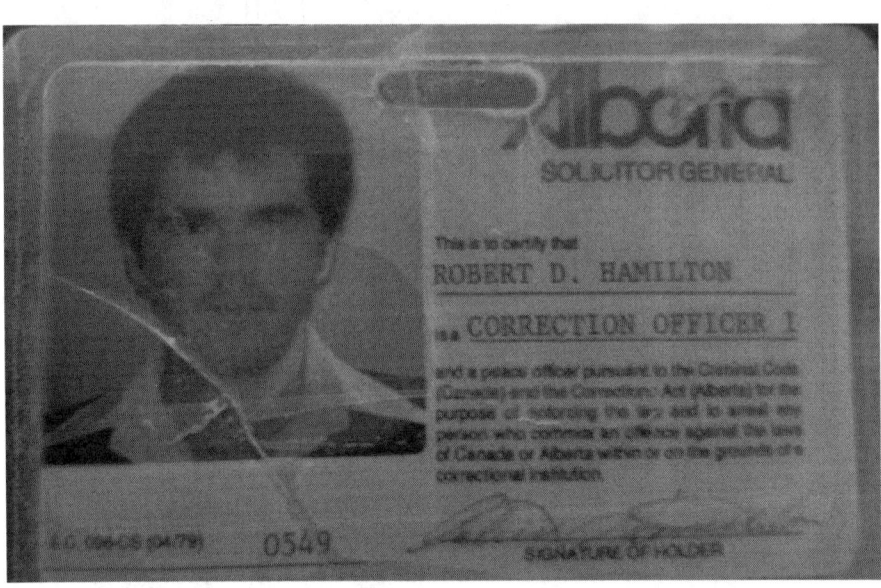

1979 Correctional Officer ID Edmonton Remand Centre

Acknowledgements

Foremost, Laney Abramson for your generosity, support, editing, and pushing me to be a better writer; James Lowewen for the use of your fabulous photo of Joe for the book cover; Pauline Silverwood for your support and encouragement; my sisters Brenda and Cindy for their love, support, and reading everything I've ever written; to The Playwright's Theatre Centre (PTC) for your support and encouragement on this project; Kim Stacey at McLaren House for your support and encouragement on this project; Angus Praught for making me aware of Renaissance Press and for your continued support as a friend; and with all my love to my mother and father for simply being them.

About the Author

Robert Hamilton spent his childhood in New Brunswick before migrating west. After a few years in Toronto and Edmonton he moved to Vancouver where he continues to live. Robert is a produced playwright with several screenplays optioned. Previously, he was Writer in Residence at the Canadian Film Centre and twice Praxis Fellow.

Renaissance was founded in May 2013 by a group of friends who wanted to publish and market those stories which don't always fit neatly in a genre, or a niche, or a demographic. We weren't sure what we wanted to publish exactly, so like the happy panbibliophiles that we are, we opened our submissions, with no other personal guideline than finding a Canadian book we would fall in love with enough that we would want to publish and sell.

Five years later, this is still very true; however, we've also noticed an interesting trend in what we tended to publish. It turns out that we are naturally drawn to the voices of those who are members of a marginalized group (especially people with disabilities and LGBTQIAPP2+ people), and these are the voices we want to continue to uplift.

To us, Renaissance isn't just a business; it's a family. Being authors and artists ourselves, we are always careful to center the experience of the author above all else.

pressesrenaissancepress.ca
pressesrenaissancepress@gmail.com

The Lemonade Series

By Jamieson Wolf

In a world filled with one-night stands, glory hole blowjobs and weeklong romances, what does it take to find love? This is just what our protagonist Blaine worries about. Unlike his friends, he wants to settle down.

pressesrenaissancepress.ca

MURDER AT THE WORLD'S FAIR
MJ LYONS

The year is 1893, and airships cloud the skies over the bustling metropolis of Toronto. The city is set to host the world's fair thanks in no small part to the work of two fantastical inventors. The New World Exhibition is to be a celebration of cultural and technological marvels; roving automatons, clockwork contraptions, the world's biggest steam-powered paddle boat, all to be fully lit by the wonder of electricity! On the day of the grand opening, young Norwood Quigley, aspiring journalist, photographer and scion of a world-famous airship magnate, stumbles onto the scene of a murder; the victim: a Prussian Ambassador; the perpetrator: a Chinese assassin, or so the powers-that-be say. In truth, the suspect is Jing, a roguish but amiable youthful delinquent. Concerned by Jing's claim of innocence and his assumed guilt by higher powers, including the British Empire's military, Norwood is thrown into a grand intrigue that hinges on Toronto's world fair. As chaos consumes the celebrations, he fears that his influential family is being manipulated in a plot to create an international incident that will lead to a war that spans the world.

pressesrenaissancepress.ca

Edited by Cait Gordon and Talia C. Johnson

We are the heroes, not the sidekicks. "Can you recommend fiction that has main characters who are like us?" This is a question we who are disabled, Deaf, neurodiverse, Spoonie, and/or who manage mental illness ask way too often. Typically, we're faced with stories about us crafted by people who really don't get us. We're turned into pathetic, tragic souls; we merely exist to inspire the abled main characters to thrive; or even worse, we're to overcome "what's wrong with us" and be cured. Nothing Without Us combines both realistic and speculative fiction, starring protagonists who are written "by us and for us." From hospital halls to jungle villages, from within the fantastical plane to deep into outer space, our heroes take us on a journey, make us think, and prompt us to cheer them on. These are bold tales, told in our voices, which are important for everyone to experience.

pressesrenaissancepress.ca

THE CYPHER

Matti McLean

Penner had always considered his life ordinary-but when his lover Chess receives a divine revelation that can't be explained, he finds himself on the run from mysterious forces.

Upending their idyllic life in a small town, Chess propels them on a journey to find answers to deep questions that plague his thoughts and his sanity.

Partnering with Fred, a boisterous sky pirate with an enigmatic past, they head out to find the answers they need on her airship. But the closer they get to their mysterious destination, the more danger they find themselves in.

Facing betrayals, battles and a malevolent being that seems to be hunting them, soon they find themselves deep into conspiracies that threaten the very fabric of their reality.

With their wits, their ship and a spot of tea, their quest for answers will make them confront the forces that created the universe.

With only each other, will their love be enough to save them?

pressesrenaissancepress.ca

A Refuge of Tales
Lynne Sargent

What does it mean to make a home inside a story? Stories are safe, comfortable, familiar. Fairytales and myths, these stories we all know and grew up with are even moreso. *A Refuge of Tales* takes everyday tropes and asks: *safe for who?* This is a collection of poems for anyone who has ever felt outside of the myth. With language both sharp and lyrical, Lynne Sargent weaves a treatise on the power of stories, and how those who have been left behind can take up that power and use it to build a new, better world.

pressesrenaissancepress.ca

Whispers Between Fairies

Derek Newman-Stille and Nathan Caro Fréchette

Fairy tales have grown with us over history and changed over the years to capture the human experience. Yet, we often trap fairy tales in the past, calling them "tradition", and it means that certain tales don't get told. Nathan Frechette and Derek Newman-Stille bring out new tales from the old, telling stories from the voices that often aren't heard.

Whispers Between Fairies is a conversation between two authors who love fairy tales and each author takes their own path to find the hidden possibilities for each fairy tale. These are tales of beauty and enchantment... but they are also tales of darkness and secrecy, much like the original fairy tales. They are echoes of the past, but also firm reminders of the magnificent diversity of the present, exploring Queer, Trans, Disabled, and Mad experiences.

Sit back and let our words be a spell that brings you to worlds of enchantment.

pressesrenaissancepress.ca

If you enjoyed this book,
consider leaving a review
where you bought it
or on a site like Goodreads!!